DAT

The Human Subject

John G. Adair

The Social Psychology of the Psychological Experiment

THE
HUMAN
SUBJECT

THE
HUMAN
SUBJECT

*The Social Psychology of the
Psychological Experiment*

JOHN G. ADAIR
University of Manitoba

 LITTLE, BROWN AND COMPANY   Boston

Library of Congress Catalog Card No. 72-14219

FIRST PRINTING

Published simultaneously in Canada
by Little, Brown & Company (Canada) Limited

PRINTED IN THE UNITED STATES OF AMERICA

To my parents
LUCIE
and
GLENN

Preface

The psychological study of human behavior typically follows a familiar course. During initial investigations, behavior appears simple, and we account for it with concise explanations such as perceptual defense, social facilitation, stimulus intensity, and anxiety. With closer study, however, we find that the behavior is complex and that our original explanations are true only under limited conditions. We realize that the focus of our study has expanded from one issue to several problems. The complexity and number of the variables we must study to account for the behavior we at first believed could be simply explained is beyond our wildest expectations.

If we charted the development of the methodology of psychology we would see that it followed a similar pattern. Psychologists design simple measures and procedures for testing hypotheses only to discover that relationships assumed to exist are complex. We learn that we may be measuring something other than what we intended or that our procedures do not convey the meaning to our subjects that they have for us. We are forced to return to the drawing board to take account of newly discovered relations.

For the past fifty years, one fundamental aspect of our methodology has resisted evolution and growth — the relationship of the human subject to the psychological experiment. Adopting the natural science model of the experimental method, we have regarded the interaction of subject, experimenter, and study as fixed and the laboratory as a methodologically sterile setting for the study of behavior. Recent research on the social psychology of the psychological experiment has proved us wrong.

Research has revealed "social contamination" in the laboratory; the subject and experimenter provide a stimulus for each other, their respective attitudes, feelings, and expectations influencing the data that are collected. This research has proposed ways to control or measure subject and experimenter bias in a study as well as alternatives to the traditional laboratory experiment. Because of its diversity, however, it is not easily interpretable, and its implications for methodological changes are not clear. This book provides an integrated view of this research and speculates on its implications for future experimentation. It is hoped that readers will gain from it a mature understanding of the experimental process, concern for its human element, and an appreciation of some of the unique controls they must exercise.

I would like to acknowledge the assistance of many who have helped make this book possible. Over the past several years, my work on the social psychology of the psychological experiment has been supported by the Canada Council, and I gratefully acknowledge their assistance. My library research was supported by Canada Council grant 69-1366, and I wrote the book while on a Canada Council Leave Fellowship. I cannot possibly mention all the individuals who helped, but I would particularly like to acknowledge the contributions of Bob Rosenthal, whose research, encouragement, and wise council have been invaluable; Martin Orne, whose research has been particularly helpful in guiding my writing; and Saul Rosenzweig, Brian Earn, and Stewart Page, who read and commented on portions of the manuscript. Finally, I would like to acknowledge the assistance of my wife, Carolyn, who not only typed the manuscript but in her way enabled the book to be completed.

Contents

A Social Psychological Analysis
of the Experiment

Pre-Experiment Attitudes
Demand Characteristics of the Experiment
Performance Cues and Subject Awareness
Role Attitude Cues and Motivation

The Cooperative Attitude
The Defensive or Apprehensive Attitude
The Negative Attitude

The Subject's Motivation: Concluding Remarks

Suggestions for Further Reading

THE
HUMAN
SUBJECT

CHAPTER ONE

Methods of Psychology:
The Spiral of History

Man's psychological processes are difficult to study. Unlike the merely reactive rat or primate, the human is a thinking, feeling organism, whose awareness of being in a study and whose thoughts about the research may affect his behavior. Psychological researchers have always had to cope with this problem. Early studies and methods emphasized the basic human characteristics of introspective awareness and verbal report. Later investigators, reacting against the subjectivity of this approach, "dehumanized" the subject by limiting their study to overt behavior examined through rigorous experimental techniques. This experimental method, borrowed from the natural sciences, has predominated for the past fifty years, but concern for a more human study of man is growing.

In contemporary research on the social psychology of the experiment, the experiment is seen as a human enterprise — an interaction of subject, experimenter, and laboratory. This research has documented that subjects are often aware of the experimenter's objectives and compliant with his demands (Orne, 1962), that the experimenter may unintentionally influence his subjects' responses (Rosenthal, 1966), that participants in experiments are usually not representative of the population at large (Rosenthal, 1965), and that, in short, the rigorous control that the psychological experiment was presumably designed to have generally does not exist. Indeed, many behavioral data may be artifacts of social interactions in the research setting rather than valid, substantive findings. This research

1

has provided a new perspective on experiments and on the potential contamination within them and is the topic to be considered here. Before turning to this subject, however, we should review its historical antecedents. An understanding of the manner in which science develops should aid this review.

The progress of scientific work is basically recurrent rather than spontaneous. Instead of a scientist's shouting "Eureka!" most scientific discoveries result from gradual increments of knowledge. The recurrent tendency in psychological research has been mentioned by Crutchfield and Krech (1962):

> We seem to detect a tendency for thinking on the problem to go full circle. But this usually turns out to be not really a circle, not simply a regression to an earlier stage. Instead, there is a kind of spiral, a recurrence of older conceptions but at a more advanced level of complexity and sophistication [p. 10].

This spiraling effect is due in part to the incremental nature of scientific discovery. Progress in science is somewhat similar to putting together a puzzle: Finding one new piece often leads to sudden advances of unusual proportions, though the immediately preceding work had seemed laborious and trivial. The history of science reveals that at times critical elements may be present, yet because of prevailing scientific thought or nonscientific events, logical increments in knowledge do not occur, though at other moments the setting is right for change and progress.

Boring (1950) has used the German word *Zeitgeist* (literally, "spirit of the times") to denote this contextual influence. He emphasizes the circumstances surrounding a scientific finding rather than the skills and knowledge of the individual scientist. A researcher occasionally may be considered a great man, but often the social context and trends of contemporary research predispose him to make his contribution. The Zeitgeist may also affect the acceptance and interpretation of innovative research. If a study is "before its time" — that is, if the Zeitgeist is not conducive to its acceptance — it may be ignored or the appropriate interpretation missed by contemporary psychologists. An understanding of the Zeitgeist is important for an understanding of the history of scientific psychology. Its influence has been considerable, and the spiral of history is apparent in the development of the methodology of psychology. A historical review of these developments will be instructive and may help us to speculate upon the next turn of the spiral — what promise this recent research in the social psychology of the experiment holds for the future.

THE EXPERIMENTAL METHOD
IN THE HISTORY OF PSYCHOLOGY

Psychology evolved from philosophy and from the natural sciences. Philosophers had long concerned themselves with problems of the mind. In the nineteenth century, British philosophers whose work had focused on the association of ideas became the forerunners of a new psychology. On the basis of their work, psychology was guided primarily to a study of the structure of consciousness — that is, to the way sensations are linked to form ideas — as its proper subject for inquiry.[1] To make its inquiry scientific, psychology borrowed from the natural sciences the rigorous experimental approach. However, because only a conscious person was capable of exploring and reporting his immediate experiences, self-observation within the experiment became the method of investigation. The new psychology thus focused on awareness — one of the attributes that separates man from other animals — and thereby recognized that the scientific study of the human organism was different from the study of other objects and required special methods.

Classical Introspection

The method and focus of psychology appeared to be designed for the unique attributes of the human subject. However, Wilhelm Wundt, the father of modern experimental psychology, used chemistry as his model for the new science. In his laboratory, the first for psychology, the experimenter was to examine the subject under a variety of conditions and to record the subject's reported conscious experiences. Wundt assumed that the investigator, much like a chemist, would search for and find the elements or mental processes that make up the structure of consciousness. According to Wundt, association provides the "glue" to combine the elements into ideas, and a breakdown or analysis by introspection will lead

[1] Psychology also had its beginnings with "non-introspective studies of reaction time, psychophysics and memory" (Woodworth, 1924, p. 258). This "objective" method was never discarded; however, the historical links with mental philosophy and Wilhelm Wundt's predilection for the introspective method and the study of consciousness clearly gave classical introspection the dominant role in psychology in the nineteenth and early in the twentieth centuries. Later, the behaviorists did not totally reject introspection. Although their treatment of it has "been decidedly amateurish" (Woodworth, 1924), they have included verbal report among their methods. Psychology has always utilized both methods in its study of the human organism. What has occurred over the years has been a shift in emphasis.

to the discovery of sensory processes as the psychological atoms of consciousness. Although Wundt's writings reveal his belief in the existence of other molecular and more complex combinations (Boring, 1953), the sensory elements of consciousness came to be the accepted level of analysis.

The subject (or observer, as he was called) was usually a psychologist or graduate student trained to make the proper observations and to report when his conscious attention deviated from the prescribed stimulus event. Wundt, it is reported (Boring, 1953), insisted on his observers' having made ten thousand introspective reactions before their data were deemed suitable for publication. The training was lengthy and intensive to ensure that the observer, much like a chemist observing reactions in a test tube, would make accurate, reliable observations:

> The observer . . . must apprehend the experimental situation, he must comprehend the rules of procedure, he must take the experimental attitude, he must intelligently understand formal instructions set him by the experimenter, he must recognize the influence upon the experimental outcome of his surroundings . . . and must detect the various and insidious forms of self-instruction which modify his reports, influence the amount of his accomplishment, and determine the character of his behavior. Finally the observer must possess the linguistic resources necessary to accurate and appropriate recital. In a word, the psychological observer is always specially and technically trained [Bentley, 1929, pp. 682–83].

The observer's status in the experiment was almost equal to that of the experimenter. The latter's role was primarily supervisory. He presented the observer with the stimulus, recorded his reports, and in general ensured that the conditions for introspection were constant. In other words, the subject provided the data that the experimenter recorded and analyzed.

The introspective report of an observer who had been presented with a bouquet of roses as a pleasant or positive affective experience (Wheeler, 1929), illustrates this process. After brief exposure to the flowers, the observer "looked" into his consciousness to recall the mental processes and sensory elements that had combined to form his experience. His observations reveal his psychological training:

> The olfactory sensation (odor) developed very suddenly to its maximum intensity; noticed at first the spicy quality then the perfume-like aroma; the rose quality itself was not analyzed at the time. Breaking in upon these olfactory experi-

ences were the muscular contractions of inhaling, and an intense wave of pleasure. Pleasantness consisted of (1) relaxed feeling of the facial muscles, especially about the eyes and mouth (relaxation of these muscles gives a peculiar quality, not like relaxation of the arm or other body muscles, and it is this quality which stands out in the pleasant experience). (2) A series of verbal remarks made to myself, "Oh, how exquisite; how delightful." (3) A most intense contraction of the diaphragm; a sinking sensation as if there were a dropping of the organs inside. The quality of this latter experience was that of strain. The whole experience startled me because I was not expecting it; it is exactly the same sort of experience I have in fear; also have experienced it in strong admiration for something, and in caressing my child. (4) General background of muscular relaxation about the trunk and legs. (5) Tendency to exhale with a sigh. The intense pleasure is the *total experience* [p. 199].

To respond in such a controlled fashion requires considerable practice. The purpose of such training and of its great duration was clear. The psychologist wanted to produce an observer who would become so habituated to the introspective method that he would report data much as a mechanical recording device records observations in other sciences (Titchener, 1912). Not all individuals are capable of developing this skill, for "there are individuals who are entirely incapable of any steady concentration of the attention, and who will therefore never make trustworthy subjects" (Wundt quoted by Titchener, 1895).

The Limitations of Introspection

The study of consciousness by introspection was not without problems. Many arose from efforts to handle the human attributes of the subject. As both the object of study and the observer, the person who made the observations was at all times aware that he was in an experiment and that the stimulus events were supposed to affect his mental experiences.

The basic concern was that the subject might not take the proper introspective attitude (*Aufgabe*) and that his observations would be inaccurate as a result of self or extraneous influence. For example, Titchener cautioned against the *stimulus error*, insisting that the observer's task was to give straightforward descriptions, without inferences about conscious data. He should report the sensory processes, not attempt to interpret them (Boring, 1953). Others cautioned against *occasional instruction*, the influence of the setting or occasion on introspective report

(Bentley, 1929; Anderson, 1930) and warned that certain *self-instructions* about the task could have unfortunate consequences on introspections (Anderson, 1930). Wundt and Titchener, however, contended that these errors were not insurmountable. Overcoming them was the purpose of the psychologist's extensive training:

> The objection overlooks the enormous influence exerted, in these as in all observations, by the mechanism of habit, by the practice which results from the frequent repetition of similar observations. *In his attention to the phenomena under observation,* the observer in psychology, no less than the observer in physics, *completely forgets to give subjective attention to the state of observing* [Wundt, quoted by Titchener, 1912, p. 413].

This answer shifted the concern to another question: What training would ensure that an observer's reports were accurate? A psychologist might observe his own mind because it is the only mind he can really know. But how could one know that his observations of his mental processes were accurate? There was no external validation. Dodge (1912) expressed his frustration about this: "If there is any way of estimating the probable error of introspection under various conditions, or any way of discovering its theoretical limitations . . . we shall have some measures of the relative certainty and finality of alleged introspective fact" (p. 215). Titchener (1912), however, countered that "In its scientific form the method is its own test; contradictory results mean an imperfect control of the conditions of observations" (p. 448). Thus, the criterion for accuracy was to be the extent to which the observer's reports were consistent with similar reports. A well-trained observer was a subject who yielded "proper" observations, that is, consistent with his training and with the theory of observation held by the investigator. Those who failed to do so were discarded, not with the intention of canceling poor data but in the belief that observations that did not conform were invalid. In one study Titchener (1895) discarded data from as many as 70 percent of his observers, for their data were "wholly irregular and inconstant."

This practice led to the well-known Titchener-Baldwin debate. Baldwin (1895) declared that the exclusion of observations because they failed to produce results desired by the investigator was an improper scientific approach. He argued that scientists could prove anything if they followed that practice. The debate centered on the use of untrained naive observers versus the use of practiced introspectionists. Baldwin believed that the former group would ensure the fair, unbiased collection of data, which presumably could be verified in other laboratories by a new group of untrained observers.

The social psychology of the psychological experiment of the 1890's and 1900's was concerned with the influence of the observer's attitude and of the laboratory setting on his responses and with the effect of his special relationship to the investigator. The observer's awareness that he was a subject in an experiment was a constant, insurmountable problem. Detractors of introspection considered the problem to be as significant a determinant of the subject's reports as were the contents of his consciousness. Wundt and Titchener and the many psychologists they influenced had tried a subjective approach to the study of what they considered a subjective problem — the study of human consciousness. They were less than successful.

Consciousness Versus Behavior

Classical introspection was also challenged because of its selection of consciousness as the subject for psychology. This topic restricted the investigations it permitted and seemed to be without any apparent functional utility (Boring, 1953). Self-observation precluded study of the retarded, the mentally ill, animal behavior, and the unconscious processes newly discovered by Freud. The value of knowing the elements of consciousness was questioned, for they had not been meaningfully related to and had not contributed much to the understanding of human behavior. This point was cogently made by Cattell, one of Wundt's former students, who said of introspectively acquired knowledge, "Such things may be ingenious and interesting . . . but we don't expect to meet them in the street" (Cattell, 1904, p. 180). He was convinced that the study of behavior in his laboratory was in no way dependent on the introspections of an observer. In his words, "It is usually no more necessary for the psychologist to be a subject than it is for the vivisected frog to be a physiologist" (p. 180). Cattell pointed out that other techniques, especially the genetic method, had made greater contributions to the knowledge of psychology than had introspection. Although he did not favor the genetic approach, those who depended on introspection rather than on the genetic approach, Cattell sarcastically noted, "still have their own genetic problem."

Following Cattell, the assault against introspection became commonplace. Within a decade, Kulpe at Wurzburg, Wertheimer and Gestalt psychology, and Watson in America successively, and with progressively greater success, challenged the classical introspection of Wundt and

Titchener. The method had been found effective in the study of sensation, perception, reaction, and memory, but Wundt had proclaimed it ineffective for the study of thought. Kulpe at the University of Wurzburg began to study thought processes under controlled conditions. He immediately discovered that the training Wundt's observers received was indeed unsuitable for the study of thought. This led to the development by one of his colleagues, Ach, of *systematic experimental introspection*, an elaborated procedure to include a *determining tendency* or attitude for the observer that enabled him to focus on the processes going on in his thinking. It also included a fractionation of the introspective period into subparts to enable the observer to cope with this sophisticated introspective problem.

Wertheimer, in devising Gestalt psychology in 1912, also reacted against introspection, and his followers eventually suggested that *phenomenological observation* replace introspection. He found that the subject perceives some experiences — mostly of an illusionary sort such as apparent movement — directly and not through the sensations of classical introspection. Thus the subject did not have to concern himself with sensations but was to report his direct phenomenal experiences. This development produced extensive experimental work on perception and illusions but did not have the dominant impact on psychology that some anticipated (Fernberger, 1937).

The Rise of Behaviorism

John B. Watson (1913) dealt the final blow to introspection and the study of consciousness. Proclaiming a radically new point of view and method for psychology, Watson believed that the time had come "when psychology must discard all reference to consciousness" (p. 163) and should develop "a purely objective experimental branch of natural science" whose "theoretical goal is the prediction and control of behavior" (p. 158). The subjectivity of consciousness and of self-observations was discarded in favor of independently verifiable observations of behavior. The subject's movements and behaviors, rather than his introspections, were the focus of the new psychology. In addition to the practical utility of studying behavior, the critical observations of the naive subject could be independently checked by various investigators under virtually identical conditions. These methods Watson sought to extend from his work in the animal laboratory to the study of human behavior. In the new behaviorism, therefore, "man and animal . . . should be placed as nearly as possible under the same experimental conditions" (p. 171).

These conditions, in particular the roles of the subject and experimenter, were in sharp contrast to those of the earlier introspective studies. In place of the highly trained, sophisticated self-observer was an untrained, naive subject who merely reacted to the manipulations and information provided by the experimenter. The experimenter became the observer and reported the new behavioral data. Only in verbal report and testing did self-observation have a place in the new psychology.

The problems posed by classical introspection were considered resolved by behaviorism. Selective subject sampling and training were dealt away by the use of naive subjects; the subjective study of consciousness was replaced by the objective study of behavior. Because the subject was no longer a trained collaborator and was treated with the objectivity accorded a laboratory rat, it was presumed that the influence of the experimenter on his results was at an end. Certainly in Watson's thinking the laboratory approach of the natural sciences, so successful in the study of animal behavior, was the ultimate in objectivity and the model for the new psychology. Many psychologists agreed.

There were some dissenters — quite a few at first, but fewer with each passing year. The model of the experimental laboratory was extended and applied with increasing skill and frequency to the study of problems in human learning, retention, transfer of training, and to the interpersonal process of social facilitation and later to studies of group climate and norm formation. The need for behavioral research was considerable, for much that had gone on before in psychology was considered of no value.

Some opposed behaviorism and its rejection of the introspective method. Many thought it was too mechanistic in its rigorous adherence to the laboratory experiment and to conditioned reflexes as the explanation for all behavior (Calkins, 1930; Bode, 1922). Although its usefulness was recognized, the rejection of subjective methods and of the unique characteristics of the human subject was deplored. As a consequence behaviorism was considered by some to be "just as one-sided as its rival and equally bizarre in its results" (Bode, 1922, p. 253). Although they pleaded for the continued use of the subjective method to complement behaviorism (Wodehouse, 1931), it was clear to many that no compromise between the two methods was possible (Pillsbury, 1922) and that the best they could hope for was a separation of psychology into independent sciences of behavior and consciousness, in which introspection had the added function of a speculative procedure to coordinate or correlate data collected from the two sciences (Fernberger, 1922).

Angell (1913) was probably the most articulate of those who counseled for moderation in passing judgment on introspection. He cautioned that the new objective methods might be competent to give rough surface fact but not in-depth knowledge. Introspection was defective, he acknowledged, but its shortcomings did not invalidate the entire technique: "Until it can be shown that introspection is totally worthless . . . it seems to me at present to afford information not to be gained elsewhere" (p. 169). In conclusion, as if he had a premonition of what the future would bring, Angell said, "Let us bid the movement toward objective description in psychology Godspeed, but let us also counsel it to forego the excesses of youth" (p. 270).

The experimental psychology of behavior began to take on polish and stature. Through operationism, introduced by the physicist Bridgman (1927), new precision was achieved. Operationism is a systematic concern for greater precision in scientific thinking, seeking to define scientific concepts in terms of the operations used to manipulate or measure them. For example, hunger might be defined operationally as twenty-three hours without food, rather than as a subjective feeling. The addition of precision to the behavioristic terminology contributed to the new science a seemingly unchallengeable scientific sophistication.

The Zeitgeist and Behaviorism

The newness, scientific respectability, achievement, and widespread acceptance of experimental behavioral psychology inhibited criticism of it. Nevertheless, it did have problems — beyond the fundamental ones operationism had resolved and much the same as those that had led to the demise of introspection. However, the discard of introspection had rid the new psychology of so many difficulties that research pointing to those that remained usually fell on deaf ears or was reinterpreted within the behaviorist framework.

Studies pointing to the problems did occasionally appear in professional journals. As early as 1925 Cason and Cason demonstrated that the behavioristic experimenter could unintentionally influence his subject's behavior. They found the experimenter's sex to be a determinant of the subject's associations to the Kent-Rossanof word list. Lipmann (1931) recognized the difficulties of obtaining a representative subject population for survey research. He observed that "since university students . . . constitute an extremely small fraction of the population . . . , they are very unsuitable subjects for research on problems pertaining to practical life" (pp. 190–91), and he attempted to establish an organization for the selection of representative samples.

The potential influence of the subject's attitude toward his task was also clearly recognized. Vernon (1934) pointed to the role of subjects' motivations and attitudes toward testing as determinants of biased data. The subject's attitude toward the hypnotist-experimenter and toward his role in the hypnotic experiment had long been recognized (Moll, 1898; Sidis, 1906). Sidis concluded that the reports and behavior of the hypnotic subject "must be taken *cum grano salis*" because his suggestability makes him "insist on what the experimenter suggests to him, whether he really experiences it or not" (Sidis, 1906, p. 240). Probably because the prevailing Zeitgeist did not include hypnotic research within the bounds of traditional experimental psychology, the similarities of compliance with the hypnotist to compliance with the experimenter was not drawn for nearly sixty years.

A similar fate was accorded the procedure suggested by Hull (1930–1931) for checking on the subject's compliance with the experimenter's hypothesis. Concerned with "hypnotic" subjects who do not go into a trance yet cooperate with the hypnotist's suggestions as if they did, Hull suggested a control procedure. The technique

> would require two squads of subjects. One would be made up of subjects who are regarded from the point of view of general behavior and reputation for honesty as being genuine. The second group would be a set of sophisticated individuals who are known not to go into a trance but who have read one or two of the modern works on hypnosis such as that of Bramwell. Have them instructed by a second experimenter to simulate the trance as best they can, with a view to deceiving the hypnotist. The subjects will all be presented to the hypnotist without distinction and he will have the task of separating the two groups by means of objective evidence. As a minimum requirement, he must not select any of the second group . . . though he might reject some of the first group, some of whom may also conceivably be simulated [p. 416].

A better description of the simulation "quasi-control" proposed by Orne (1962) as a means of assessing the subjects' compliance could not be found. Developed for hypnosis in 1931, this technique did not appear to have relevance to the new psychology.

Even in the conditioning experiment, a prominent element in behavioristic research, artifacts of the research process were recognized. Noting the greater speed and regularity of responses in simple reaction-time experiments than those in conditioned hand withdrawal, Cason (1934) speculated that this was due to the fact that subjects in the former studies are told precisely what they are supposed to do whereas the subject in the conditioning task may not know he is supposed to do anything. Cason concluded that people learn better when they know what they are supposed to learn; thus verbal activities in human motor learning must be taken into account: "It does not seem a defensible scientific method to limit one's self to a behaviorist description of the hand when the psychological processes which have afforded a fairly satisfactory explanation of what the hand does are located elsewhere in the body" (p. 571). The unique verbal abilities of the human subject, however, are ignored because psychologists often "assume that the people who act as subjects for us are animals, or at least . . . treat them as if they were animals" (p. 564).

Often the prevailing Zeitgeist led to interpretations of laboratory artifacts as *support* for the behaviorist framework. For example, in one study the subject's galvanic skin response (a decreased electrical resistance of the skin accompanying a heightened emotional response) was found to occur to a signal light on the first trial when the subject was told he would receive an electric shock following the stimulus (Cook and Harris, 1937). The effect of the subject's awareness of experimental conditions was interpreted as evidence for one-trial *verbal conditioning*. To interpret it otherwise would have been counter to the prevailing Zeitgeist.

These examples show that there was recognition of the inadequacies of the traditional experimental model. The criticisms were fractionated, however, and the ease with which a single instance of artifact could be rationalized added to its relative lack of influence. On the other hand, the brilliant analysis of the social nature of the laboratory experiment by Saul Rosenzweig (1933) did not fare any better. With considerable care and much insight, in his first published paper, the young psychologist analyzed "the experimental situation as a psychological problem." He made this contribution on the basis of a program of research devoted to the experimental validation of certain psychoanalytic concepts. The analysis grew out of Rosenzweig's extensive empirical observations and was augmented by a survey of previous work. He defined three errors or influences in psychological experimentation that render it more difficult than research in the established physical sciences. The first of these, *errors of observational attitude*, were peculiar to the introspective study and more or less equivalent to Titchener's stimulus error.

The second difficulty, *errors of motivational attitude,* has applicability to both the introspective and the behavioral experiment. It arises from the subject's awareness and questioning attitude toward the experiment:

> A subject who acts in this way commits what we shall call the "opinion-error": he entertains opinion about the experiment —

what its purpose is and what he may reveal in it — instead of simply reacting in a naive manner. The causes of the opinion-error are usually certain motives, such as curiosity and pride [p. 343].

Rosenzweig's description of the opinion error is similar to the concept of demand characteristics (Orne, 1962), which had such an impact on research thirty years later (see Chapter 2). The similarity is even greater when one considers that Rosenzweig, like Orne, suggested that compliance or cooperation with the experimenter's hypothesis may be motivated by a desire to save the experimenter's self-respect.[2] It is interesting that pride, as a motive for the opinion error, is virtually identical to Rosenberg's conception of evaluation apprehension (see Chapter 2), which also appeared much later:

> Pride causes the Ee [subject] to reflect about his behavior in the experimental situation and then to modify it in accordance with certain opinions that arise in his mind as a result of these reflections. The object of such modifications is usually to save the face of the subject. He naturally wants not to appear stupid or ill-bred or greedy or immoral, and so forth [1933, p. 344].

To counter errors of motivational attitude Rosenzweig suggested procedures designed to maintain the naiveté of the subject — for example, the use of child subjects or strong stimuli that elicit natural behavior. He felt that the subject's awareness might also be reduced by misleading him about the object of the study. Deception is a common procedure in contemporary psychology; in 1933 it was somewhat novel and, according to Rosenzweig, "not always pleasant at first." Provided he is certain he will not injure his subject by the deception, the experimenter may "solace himself with the consideration that the scientific end justify the scientific means" (p. 349). As an alternative, Rosenzweig suggested that the experimenter "interogate the subject after the experiment as to the opinions he entertained" (p. 350), to assess errors of motivational attitude much as the contemporary use of the post-experimental questionnaire does (see Chapter 6).

With uncanny thoroughness Rosenzweig turns to the experimenter as the source of the third difficulty — *errors of personality influence*. He distinguishes two errors. First, the experimenter's personal qualities, such

2 The similarity of Rosenzweig's concepts to those of today was noted by Silverman and Shulman (1970); however, that the position taken by the contemporary work on the social psychology of the experiment had been outlined by Rosenzweig was recognized much earlier (Lyons, 1964).

as his race or sex, may influence the subject's behavior (this is comparable to the experimenter effects discussed in Chapter 3). The second, called *suggestion error,* is virtually identical to the experimenter expectancy effects (also discussed in Chapter 3). Rosenzweig wrote:

> It is not difficult to see how an unguarded word, or glance from the Er [Experimenter], may have a suggestive significance of marked consequence to certain experimental results. . . . The sensitivity in this regard of human subjects is obviously even greater than that of animals [pp. 352–53].

This sensitivity to the experimenter's potential yet subtle influence was a significant advance in thinking on the social psychology of the experiment. Here in a single paper in 1933 was a concise yet thorough analysis of the experiment as a social situation. Unfortunately, this splendidly critical analysis was ahead of its time; the challenge to reconsider aspects of the research method was not met. Instead of pursuing these concerns and documenting instances of artifact, Rosenzweig himself felt that "once the inevitable ingredients of the experimental situation had been recognized, the important thing was to move on to research incorporating these insights and attempting to systematically include them as *parameters* of the experimental-social situation." [3] This new approach, called *experimental idiodynamics* (Rosenzweig, 1952), was not widely accepted. The Zeitgeist was still not right, and Rosenzweig's insights remained buried for thirty-five years.[4]

Through the next two decades and more, concerns with methodological difficulties were expressed and ignored, documented and forgotten. Brower (1948), in one of the earliest studies of volunteer and non-volunteer effects in laboratory research, demonstrated that subjects performing under a system of compulsory participation yielded data different from those of volunteers. Hyman (1954) began to be concerned with the effects of personal differences between interviewers on their survey data, and occasional concerns about examiner effects appeared in the testing literature (Lord, 1950). McKinney (1955) examined subjects' reactions to deception. In 1956 Brunswick questioned the ecological validity of

---

[3] Personal communication, 1970.

[4] Ironically, a personal encounter with the Zeitgeist and with E. G. Boring, who introduced this notion to psychology, was experienced by Rosenzweig. In a memorial to Boring, his department chairman in 1933, Rosenzweig (1970) recalls Boring's opposition to his use of the novel term *experimentee* as a substitute for both subject and observer. Rosenzweig yielded to Boring's formidable opposition on this trivial point in the larger context of his significant program on behavioral research. But, Rosenzweig recalled, "the context was lost on him and, as representative of the predominant Zeitgeist, he prevailed" (p. 68).

laboratory research — that is, the extent to which the phenomena studied in the experiment were generalizable to the world outside the laboratory. He was particularly concerned with the peculiarities of the laboratory setting and of the typical samples studied. These important individual efforts, however, did not change and improve research methodology.

THE SOCIAL PSYCHOLOGY OF THE EXPERIMENT IN CONTEMPORARY PSYCHOLOGY

Not until the 1950's did the Zeitgeist begin to change. The honeymoon with behaviorism came to an end as problems were increasingly encountered in the application of its methods to complex behaviors. The problems first became troublesome on a large scale in social and clinical psychology, where the incongruity of applying the rigorous methods originally developed for the study of animal behavior to the study of socially relevant human behaviors was most evident. This is reflected in the research interests of the investigators who have made the most significant contributions to understanding of socially derived artifacts — hypnosis (Orne), social-clinical psychology (Rosenthal), and attitude change (Rosenberg). In these areas the subject's awareness of the experiment's purposes became a central concern, and deception was tried as a solution. From these difficulties contemporary research on the social psychology of the psychological experiment emerged.

The critical and sometimes anti-intellectual Zeitgeist of the 1960's also contributed to the need for reexamination of the social aspects of research. This climate, reflected in the student power and civil rights movements and in other challenges to the establishment, encouraged questioning of the relevance of traditional disciplines and their methods. Indeed, it has been called by some the "age of relevance" (Silverman, 1971). In this context the relevance of traditional institutions such as education, law, and standards of conduct has been subjected to a critical reappraisal, and the research topics and methodology of psychology have not escaped this scrutiny. Undergraduates in particular have demanded answers to difficult, socially relevant questions, and agencies that fund research have also become interested in social problems. That experimental psychology has had difficulty and is apparently unable to satisfactorily answer many of the questions has added to the growing impression that to a large extent research methods have lacked relevance (Silverman, 1971).

Although originating in *social* psychology and stimulated by the need for research with *social* relevance, research and criticisms of methodology are not limited to the *social* psychological experiment. The problems of social artifact in basic research in the laboratory-bound disciplines of learning and experimental psychology are similar to those found elsewhere. They have been, however, somewhat less obvious, and consequently investigators in these areas are more reluctant to acknowledge their presence. As research in what some psychologists call the "soft" areas presents unchallengeable evidence of the social influences on the laboratory experiment, the Zeitgeist within the traditional experimental psychology as a whole may change.

In spite of the reluctance of experimental psychologists, the Zeitgeist of the 1960's and 1970's has stimulated extensive research on the social psychology of the experiment and a reexamination of the methods of psychology. The impact of this research on the future of the laboratory experiment is uncertain. Nevertheless, evidence suggests that it and the prevailing Zeitgeist may stimulate a new turn in the spiral of history. Before assessing the evidence and possibilities for the future, we shall examine the critical research on the social psychology of the experiment.

SUGGESTIONS FOR FURTHER READING

Historical Background

Crutchfield, R. S., and Krech, D. 1962. Some guides to the understanding of the history of psychology. In *Psychology in the making,* ed. L. Postman, pp. 3–27. New York: Knopf.

The authors provide a perspective of the cultural and scientific context of discovery in which the spiraling history of psychology may be appreciated.

Boring, E. G. 1963. The Zeitgeist and the psychology of science. In *History, psychology and science: selected papers by Edwin G. Boring,* ed. R. I. Watson and D. T. Campbell, pp. 1–108. New York: Wiley.

In this collection of Boring's writing, the roles of the Zeitgeist and of the great man in the history of psychology are explored.

Introspection

Boring, E. G. 1953. A history of introspection. *Psychological bulletin* 50: 169–89.

This article is a review of the development, application, and declining use of introspection as a method of psychological research.

Vanderplas, J. M., ed. 1966. *Controversial issues in psychology,* pp. 135–90. Boston: Houghton Mifflin.

The relevant section of this collection of readings is entitled "The Reaction Time." Reprinted are the major papers of the Titchener-Baldwin debate over whether the subjects should be highly trained or naive.

The Behavioristic Experiment

Rosenzweig, S. 1933. The experimental situation as a psychological problem. *Psychological review* 40: 337–54.

In this careful analysis of the difficulty of studying human behavior, methodological errors that occur in both behavorial and introspective study and methods to deal with them are explored.

Friedman, N. 1967. *The social nature of psychological research: the psychological experiment as a social interaction,* pp. 3–34. New York: Basic Books.

The focus of this historical survey of the research methods of psychology is the experimenter's role and his relation to the subject. Friedman's major theme is that the experimenter's interpersonal contribution to the experiment has been largely ignored.

Schultz, D. P. 1969. The human subject in psychological research. *Psychological bulletin* 72: 214–28.

In this historical survey of subjects' changing role in the psychological experiment, the implications of the way in which the subject is currently treated are explored.

CHAPTER TWO

The Social Nature of Behavioral Research:
The Subject's Awareness
and Motivation

The form of the laboratory experiment, the source of the major portion of our systematic knowledge in psychology, is somewhat traditional. It may be described as an interaction of a subject and an experimenter taking place within a closed environment. Unlike the laboratories of the natural sciences, the behavioral laboratory may not be considered "sterile." A psychological experiment is influenced by the thoughts, feelings, attitudes, and intentions of both subject and researcher. Through subtle interpersonal influence the behavior of one participant may unintentionally and covertly alter the behavior of the other. The bias of data that results from this influence often goes undetected. The interpersonal nature of the experiment makes the study of human behavior difficult, but the continuation of biased research is largely due to investigators' insensitivity to the subject's thoughts and feelings. Their failure to consider that the subject's perception of his role in the experiment may contrast sharply with what they intended it to be is a significant source of bias.

THE RESEARCHER'S VIEW OF HIS EXPERIMENT

To the investigator who has been trained in the tradition of the laboratory an experiment consists of selected experiences ("slices of life") examined under rigorously controlled conditions. The experimenter plays a prominent role in the examination. He typically provides the subject with information and with a stimulus event that he has carefully manipulated. He simultaneously controls many other relevant variables and observes and records the subject's reactions.

The subject is generally not considered to be active in the research process; his role vis-à-vis the experiment and the experimenter is limited and clearly prescribed. He is treated like a research object that is expected to naively provide behavioral data in response to manipulations and instructions. His thoughts and feelings about the research are seldom taken into account and then only after the experiment to verify previous manipulations. The subject may actively seek answers to his questions about the experiment, discover the hypothesis the experimenter is testing, and respond with insight rather than naiveté to the manipulations, but this is not what the experimenter intended and it is inconsistent with the traditional research model.

Nevertheless, the subject's role is a persistent concern of the investigator. He has been trained to assume that subjects will react somewhat naturally in the laboratory, yet in most studies he knows they are aware of being in an experiment and may even be aware of his hypothesis. He hopes that his study will be so stimulating and involving that their awareness will not be a problem or, if his concerns persist, he may be forced to the often-used, untested rationalization that "the subject's thoughts won't make any difference anyway." If he does not talk to his subjects — unfortunately the habit of many investigators — his rationalization is unchallenged and the "validity" of his experiment is assured. By querying his subjects, he would have found that their view of his experiment was entirely different from his own.

THE SUBJECT'S VIEW OF THE EXPERIMENT

A person who agrees for the first time to serve in an experiment probably does so somewhat reluctantly. Psychologists are supposed to be able to explore one's mind, thoughts, and feelings, but exactly how they conduct their scientific research is not common knowledge. Nevertheless, someone who has agreed to be in a scientific experiment, which might be significant, probably feels important and eager to perform well.

The subject arrives at the laboratory somewhat apprehensive and tense. Little about the situation makes him change his feelings. The room is cold and rather sterile. The experimenter in his white lab coat is not diffident, but his businesslike manner does nothing to reduce apprehension. The subject feels particularly uncomfortable because he knows little about the experiment. He was not told much when he agreed to participate, and there is not a great deal in the room to indicate what he is going to have to do.

In the first few moments the subject visually and mentally explores the room in an attempt to size up the experimenter and his equipment and determine what the study is to be about. At first glance there does not appear to be anything frightening. There are no hypodermic needles, shock boxes, or long couches with subdued lighting. The experimenter appears competent, but he does not seem threatening.

When the experimenter begins to read the instructions, the subject probably thinks to himself, "Now I'll find out what it's all about." But the experimenter does not give all the answers. The subject is told he is to learn a list of words presented by a slide projector. He thinks, "I can certainly do that, but what is the purpose of the other words the experimenter says he will simultaneously present on the tape recorder?" The subject's mental hypotheses begin to develop: "Am I to learn those as well, or is that merely a distraction? But why would he use single words as a distraction? I'll bet . . ."

The first few words do not register well. The subject is still half thinking about the experiment and trying to decide what he is to do. Although he begins to give them more attention, he is still trying to formulate a hypothesis: "The experimenter said it was to see how well I could learn a list of written words, but there is something about the way he said it that didn't sound as if he really meant it. Besides, the words on the tape recorder seem to have something in common. That's it! About half of them are happy, positive words; others seem to be negative like *ugly, dirty*, and so on." The subject listens further and realizes what the experimenter is doing. Happy, pleasant words are always paired with the same words on the projected list and the same is true of the negative words. The experiment is to see if the subject will think the projected words more positive if they are paired with pleasant words all the time and have the opposite feeling toward the other words. It's like the conditioning process that the subject read about in the introductory textbook.

The subject's insights and mental hypotheses develop gradually as he views each of the words. He pieces together what the experimenter says and the way he says it, the words presented on the tape recorder and by the projector, what he has read about psychology, and his notions about what a psychologist in a university might be studying. He concludes what he thinks the experiment was about and is prepared to act on his hypothesis.

The subject never really considers not doing what is asked of him. He has agreed to assist the experimenter, and in this case that means learning the words paired with both happy-sounding and negative-sounding words. The subject would like to see whether he can do it well. The experiment is like a challenging game, and the subject thinks, "Maybe when it's over he will tell me if I was right." So the subject does his best to learn the words, and when the experimenter asks at the end of the experiment, he proudly recalls as many from both lists as he can. When the experimenter then asks the subject to evaluate the projected words on a scale from pleasant to unpleasant, he knows his hypothesis was correct. He solved the problem the experimenter posed for him, and his responses confirmed the experimenter's hypothesis.

This fictitious experiment was designed to study the classical conditioning of affective meaning — that is, the degree of feeling tone for a particular word that could develop with its frequent and consistent association with other words that were positively or negatively toned. The experimenter intended that after repeated pairings the subject would rate the words that had positive associations as being more pleasant than those that had been paired with negative words. He had hoped that if the subject's attention was focused on learning the projected list he would not notice the relationship between the sets of words. The experimenter expected to demonstrate a verbal conditioning process with human subjects much like Pavlov's classic demonstration of salivary conditioning with dogs.

The discrepancy between the subject's perception and what the experimenter intended is considerable. He assumed the subject would passively react to the appropriate stimulus event; the subject viewed the experiment as a problem to which he actively sought a solution. From his data the experimenter might deduce that the subject gradually acquired a positive feeling toward certain words through a subtle form of conditioning. However, a realistic appraisal of the experiment from the subject's perspective would reveal a cognitive process of problem solution.

For scientific purposes, which view of the experiment is more valid, the subject's or the experimenter's? Obviously we must consider the subject's understandings of the experiment. We are studying *his* behavior in response to *his* perception of the experimental situation. In this sense, the subject may determine his part in the experiment. His perceptions, choice of responses, and willingness to cooperate with the experimenter give the active subject a much greater role than was intended. The investigator has less absolute control over the experimental process than many have casually assumed. Although he may operationally define his manipulations and measures, the subject's perception of them gives them meaning.

Just as the subject is a more active participant than he has been thought to be, so must the psychologist become a more versatile researcher. To restore much of his advantage in this interaction, the investigator must understand the subject's active participation and the processes by which he responds to the experiment. To do so requires an examination of what contributes to the subject's behavior in the experiment.

A SOCIAL PSYCHOLOGICAL ANALYSIS OF THE EXPERIMENT

Because we are primarily concerned with the subject's behavior, our analysis will focus on *his* attitudes, intentions, and interactions. The interaction may be conceptualized into an *experimental situation* to which the subject responds — for example, the laboratory, the experimenter, and the task — and the *subject's contribution* to the experiment — his attitudes, sets, and motivations. These parallel the two related problems of awareness and motivation created by an active subject. On the one hand his *awareness* of the hypothesis destroys the naiveté the experimenter intended. Equally troublesome is the subject's *motivation* to take a problem-solving approach to the experiment and to confirm or disconfirm the experimenter's hypothesis. Confirmation of the hypothesis merely because the subject wanted to help is not the scientific result we are looking for. An examination of these problems reveals that awareness and motivation cannot be considered independent of each other. Indeed our concern in this analysis is with the interaction of the subject's cognitions (thoughts) and motivations within the experimental context.

Pre-Experiment Attitudes

Although the traditional experimental model assumes that subjects' prior experiences will be randomly distributed among various treatment groups and will not systematically influence the data, it is unrealistic to assume that subjects will enter an experiment totally unbiased. They have prior thoughts and feelings about research in general, and their predisposition to approach an experiment in a uniform manner affects their responses. In general two initial or pre-experiment attitudes should be noted.

An inquiring or problem-solving attitude is common and strongly motivated in many subjects. In part it may arise from a need to provide structure to a totally new experience. Subjects are also concerned, to some extent, that they perform adequately so that the study will be successful or so they will "look good" to the experimenter. They do not want their participation to be a waste of time or to receive a poor evaluation. To prevent this requires that they know what the study is about. Also, by volunteering for an experiment the subject may feel he has contracted to cooperate with the experimenter in the study itself. To do this may require knowledge of the study beyond that contained in the instructions. Hence, immediately upon entering the laboratory the subject seeks the somewhat hidden structure and meaning of the experiment and continues active problem-solving as he receives added insights.

In addition to this problem-solving set subjects typically have an attitude toward psychological research in general that may vary along a continuum from positive to somewhat negative. Attitudes about the scientific study of behavior may influence their thoughts, behaviors, or motivations. In general, subjects with positive attitudes should be perceptive and responsive to psychological research. This is illustrated by the greater awareness of the hypothesis by subjects with positive attitudes in a series of studies of verbal conditioning, conformity, and attitude change (Adair, 1970a, 1970b, 1972a; Adair and Fenton, 1971). Because their positive attitudes predisposed them to volunteer for a study (Adair, 1970b) or to enroll in an introductory psychology course in which they are required to participate in experiments, cooperation in the study itself should be another manifestation of their positive attitudes. This was found in a study of attitude change (Adair and Fenton, 1971) in which change increased as the subjects' attitudes toward psychological research became more positive.

Both of these pre-experiment attitudes provide the basis for the subjects' motivations and cognitions about the experiment. Subjects with the most positive attitudes are initially predisposed to cooperate with the experimenter, and their desire to cooperate and problem-solving attitudes sensitize them to cues in the experimental situation that may signal what they are to do.

Demand Characteristics of the Experiment

Once the subject is in the laboratory, certain features of the situation will have a greater influence on his understanding than will others. For example, in the study just reviewed, the instructions, the experimenter's voice, the apparatus, and the subject's notions of what psychologists study contributed to the development by the subject of a conditioning hypothesis. This led him to attend to and rehearse certain words and to ignore others. Orne (1962) terms the characteristics of the experimental situation that indicate a particular response to the subject *demand characteristics*. Defined as the "totality of cues to which the subject responds that influence his behavior in the experiment," they include treatments or manipulations as well as any extraneous features within the experiment. Rumors and other prior information about the study may also be regarded as demand characteristics. Although originally intended to account for the subject's development of an awareness of the hypothesis that he would cooperatively confirm, the concept of demand characteristics has been broadened to designate all cues in the experiment that may influence the subject. For example, the subject need not be aware that he has been cued by demand characteristics to respond in a particular way, nor is he required to confirm the hypothesis he perceives as correct. Indeed certain demand characteristics in the experiment may alter his attitude so that he is motivated to disconfirm the hypothesis. In our analysis demand characteristics will be used in this broad sense.

It will be conceptually useful to subdivide this generic concept into functional units related to attitudes and performance. On the one hand cues in the experiment may signal a hypothesis or elicit a particular response from the subject. These will be designated *performance cues*.[1] On the other hand certain demand characteristics may modify the subject's motivation. These *role attitude cues*, such as the treatments or the attitude of the experimenter, may reinforce or signal the need for a shift in the initial attitude of the subject to one more consistent with his new role in the experiment. The two sets of cues interact, but we shall first examine them separately.

Performance Cues and Subject Awareness

Performance cues are the features of the experiment that define for the subject the specific responses he is to make. They can accomplish this in one of two ways. First, the cues may provide the necessary information for cognitively structuring the experiment and developing a hypothesis. Instigated by his problem-solving set, the subject seeks out the performance cues that will signal what the experiment is about. The subject-created hypothesis determines the specific responses he will decide to make.

[1] This term was first used by Weber and Cook (1972). It has the meaning in the present context that they assigned it.

This is illustrated in a study (Adair, 1970) in which perception of contrasting performance cues led subjects to opposing behaviors. The study was examining motor skills and involved twenty-five one-minute trials on the pursuit rotor and some hand dynamometer measures. The pursuit rotor requires the subject to maintain contact between a pencil-like stylus held in his hand and a target on a rotating turntable. The dynamometer measures the strength of grip. At the conclusion of the session subjects were asked what they had perceived to be the experiment's purpose and what effect the twenty-five trials following the target on the pursuit rotor were to have had on their performance. Most subjects perceived it as a motor learning task and believed that with practice they were to get better at keeping the stylus on the target. The task, instructions, and number of trials guided their development of this hypothesis. In contrast a number of subjects reported an alternative hypothesis — that the experiment was a study of the effects of fatigue and that their performance was expected to stay the same or deteriorate. Presumably the combination of dynamometer measures with pursuit rotor trials and the repetitious nature of the task were salient to these subjects. Performance cues had led both groups of subjects to conflicting hypotheses, with the result that "learners" performed at a significantly higher level of accuracy than did subjects who had perceived the fatigue hypothesis.

In a second way, performance cues may directly alter the subject's behavior without his awareness. The experimenter's unintentional influence on his subject (to be discussed in the next chapter) is a good example of this. Consider a study in which the subjects were tested in a verbal learning task by one of several experimenters (Winkel and Sarason, 1964). Prior test results revealed that half of the experimenters had scored high on a measure of test anxiety and that the others were relatively nonanxious. It was found that the level of the experimenter's test anxiety significantly influenced the subjects' performance. Female subjects performed best when tested by the nonanxious rather than by the extremely anxious experimenter. Female subjects were inferior to males under reassurance instructions read by highly anxious experimenters; yet the reverse was true with low-anxious experimenters. Presumably the anxiety levels of the experimenters served as performance cues to which subjects unconsciously responded with different rates of verbal learning.

The data or responses the experimenter desires or expects may similarly be translated into performance cues that influence the subject's behavior without their awareness. It has been found that subjects will rate photographs positively or negatively if the experimenter appropriately varies the emphasis in his speech or gives other cues to signal the desired response (Duncan and Rosenthal, 1968). Because subjects are unaware of these subtle demand characteristics, it is often difficult to specify such contamination of psychological research.

Role Attitude Cues and Motivation

The subject enters the experiment with an attitude that predisposes him to respond positively or negatively to the manipulations. Because most have positive attitudes, at first they are generally motivated to cooperate with the instructions. As the study progresses and the subject learns more about the experiment and his role in it, however, certain demand characteristics tend to reinforce or change his initial attitude. If he finds the experimenter pleasant, the room neat, the instructions clear and interesting, and the task absorbing, his cooperative attitude will likely be reinforced. However, he may be kept waiting for the experiment to start, find the experimenter unpleasant or deceiving, and feel he is belittled by the task. In this case the role attitude cues transform his initial predisposition to cooperate to a negative attitude. This determines how the subject will respond to the performance cues that have signaled the hypothesis. Although the subject may be motivated in various ways, three role attitudes appear to be typical.

The Cooperative Attitude. The desire to cooperate with the experimenter's hypothesis is common among subjects and appears to guide their behavior in all studies where there are no compelling cues to the contrary. The relationship between subject and experimenter contributes to the frequent occurrence of this motive. In addition to positive pre-experiment attitudes, the act of volunteering or signing up for an experiment seals a personal contract between the experimenter and the subject, fostering cooperative behavior. The experimenter often fails to enlighten the subject about his continuing role; thus the subject is unsure how he is to behave when the experiment begins. In the absence of instructions to the contrary, he surmises that the initial contract implies an obligation to cooperate with the investigator during the study. The subject's reluctance to waste his time by not fulfilling his part of the bargain also strengthens his cooperative attitude.

Orne (1962) has suggested that the subject is inclined to cooperate because of a desire to contribute to the advancement of science. The subject feels that he will further the aims of science by his participation in a university research project. The demand characteristics he experiences in his initial exposure to the experiment — elaborate equipment, laboratory setting, the presence of the experimenter, sometimes dressed in a white lab coat — tend to reinforce the expectation that the experiment is truly scientific. According to Orne, the almost universal strategy of subjects, based on their high "regard for the aims of science and experimentation" and a strong motivation to play the role of a "good" subject, is to cooperate with the experimenter by validating his hypothesis.

The extent of this cooperative attitude is reflected in Orne's efforts (1962) to find a laboratory task that subjects would not willingly perform. He wanted to test the commonly held notion that persons could not be induced to perform a distasteful task even under hypnosis. Subjects were given a stack of two thousand mimeographed sheets and a pack of 3 x 5 cards. They were asked to compute the more than two hundred additions of numbers on the first sheet and then to read the top 3 x 5 card for further instructions. The printed card told them to tear the sheet of additions they had just completed into not less than thirty-two pieces and to compute them again on the next mimeographed page. They were then to turn to the next card for further instructions. Because subjects would quickly realize that all cards contained the same instructions and that the task was meaningless, it was expected that they would work only a short time and then quit. Surprisingly, however, the experimenter had to stop each subject after several hours of work. Unlike the experimenter, the subjects had seen meaning in the task. They had perceived it as a test of their endurance and had shown incredible willingness to work hard to fulfill the requirements of this scientific study.

Orne (1962) reflected the strength of the cooperative attitude in his selection of the term *demand characteristics* to describe the cues in the experiment that guide behavior. If subjects are so strongly motivated to cooperate, these characteristics *demand* certain behaviors rather than merely convey information. The apparent strength of this motive leads him to conclude that for subjects to behave in a manner contrary to the experimenter's hypothesis, they must misperceive the demand characteristics or the hypothesis must be so obvious that the subjects' desires to further science dictate that they "bend over backwards" to give an honest response. In other words, the subject will respond noncooperatively only when his perception of the situation changes, not because he is differently motivated. Although Orne (1969) admits that subjects may be motivated in other ways, his emphasis on the cooperative tendency has highlighted the predominant motive among subjects.[2]

---

[2] Orne's emphasis on the cooperative subject is understandable. His studies of hypnosis, itself a somewhat cooperative process, employ volunteer subjects who must travel some distance to arrive at his laboratory. Moreover, he is an excellent researcher who takes great care in preparation of his subjects. Under these conditions he rarely, if ever, sees a noncooperative subject.

The importance of the subject's awareness of the hypothesis and his cooperative motive is found in the psychological research in which it has been shown to have an effect. In addition to the subject's compliance in sensory deprivation (Orne and Scheibe, 1964) and in classical conditioning of attitudes (Page, 1969), cooperative subject motivation has been evident in studies of the cue value of aggressive stimuli (Page and Scheidt, 1971), verbal operant conditioning (Mondy, 1968; Holmes, 1967), observational learning (Hamilton, Thompson, and White, 1970), treatment for insomnia (Eisenman, 1970), and in ratings of consumer products (Jacoby, Olson, and Haddock, 1971). In each study the subjects knew what the experimenter wanted and were willing to cooperate. For example, in the product-rating study subjects were to rate the quality of three different beer samples, and they ranked them as expected, according to the brand names, though all the samples were of the same beer. The strength of the cooperative motive is most strongly revealed, however, in the behavior of Orne's subjects who willingly tore up each sheet of their math calculations immediately after completing them and repeated this behavior for seven hours.

The Defensive or Apprehensive Attitude. The subject often approaches the laboratory worried and concerned (Gustav, 1962). The experiment may suggest that it is designed to evaluate him personally, and his apprehension is easy to understand. Psychologists are generally thought to possess a special ability to analyze a person's needs, feelings, and thoughts after a brief encounter. Simply tell someone you are majoring in psychology or that you are a psychologist and watch their reaction. It will probably resemble the experience Marshall Segal (1965) had at a tribal crowning ceremony in central Africa. Atop a hill, with the cries of wild animals in the surrounding fields, Dr. Segal was introduced to a Congo chieftain who had come to the ceremony from more than two hundred miles away. He was introduced as a psychologist, to which the Congo chieftain, with the expression common at cocktail parties the world over, replied, "I presume, Dr. Segal, that before this party is over you will have psychoanalyzed me." This thought is widespread, and it is certain that most subjects encountering a psychologist in his laboratory will experience some of this concern.

When the subject enters the experiment, there are cues to reinforce his initial expectations, particularly if measures of his abilities, capabilities, attitudes, or personal traits are made. Such tests are salient role attitude cues that almost always evoke concern about one's performance. Moreover, most behaviors studied by psychologists serve a similar function.

Obtaining the subjects' reactions to aggression, dependency, altruism, or conformity pressure inevitably conveys a certain degree of evaluative anxiety and stimulates efforts to look good — that is, to adopt a defensive or apprehensive role attitude.

Although the subject's desire to "put his best foot forward" has been considered a prime motive for some time (Rosenzweig, 1933; Riecken, 1962), the concept of evaluation apprehension and its theoretical and empirical support have been developed more recently by Rosenberg (1965). He first introduced the concept as an alternative to much of the attitude change effects found when subjects are asked to write counter-attitudinal essays. Cognitive dissonance theory predicts that subjects who receive a small justification (reward) for writing an essay counter to their own attitude will experience more dissonance and hence show greater change toward the position taken in their essay than subjects paid a larger reward. They apparently do not feel sufficiently rewarded and must reconcile the inconsistency in their behavior by a subsequent change in attitude. High-reward subjects, on the other hand, feel that the unusually large payment justifies their behavior and they have no need to change. The predicted results have been obtained in a number of studies, but an alternative interpretation is plausible. Rosenberg suggests that the surprisingly large reward may have appeared to the high-reward subjects as a bribe to see if their attitudes could be "bought." This would have cued them to a defensive role attitude and to less attitude change to show the experimenter they could not be bribed. By replicating the dissonance study with alteration in the procedure to eliminate the evaluation apprehension, Rosenberg was able to demonstrate a different result.

He removed the role attitude cues by separating the dependent measure of the subjects' attitudes from the setting in which the counter-attitudinal manipulation had taken place. In other words, subjects wrote the essay in one experiment and were asked their attitude toward that object quite incidentally as part of another study. In this way the evaluative concern aroused by the manipulations was not present when their attitudes were measured and was not a determinant of their response. This important new approach in research design should be employed whenever cues for evaluative anxiety may be present. Its use in dissonance studies has permitted greater confidence in the interpretation of their data.

The altered replication demonstrated what would happen if certain cues were removed from an experiment. The effects of role attitude have also been documented in studies where evaluation apprehension was intentionally aroused. Rosenberg (1969) has surveyed several, and one may serve as an example. In it, evaluative concern was produced by reminding subjects of their freshman tests before they were given another series of brief ability tests. They were asked to tap a key with their right and then with their left index finger. Ordinarily tapping rates are greater for the preferred finger. However, the experimenter told these subjects that graduate students at Yale and Michigan had been found to tap the key at similar rates with each index finger, implying a relationship with intelligence. In comparison with the rates of control subjects who did not receive these instructions, the difference in tapping rates for the two fingers was significantly less for the apprehensive subjects. Although the study is simple, the results underscore subjects' need to obtain a favorable evaluation from the experimenter.

The role of evaluation apprehension in research has been recognized primarily in studies of forced compliance and attitude change that have been designed to test dissonance theory. The apprehensive role attitude, however, is readily aroused in a variety of contexts and should be a potent source of subject bias. For example, it may account for the phenomenon of social facilitation. This is the observation that the presence of an audience enhances the emission of dominant responses and leads to a performance superior to the one subjects would have given had they been alone. Indeed, superior performance has been found to occur with or without an audience only by subjects who anticipated evaluation (Paulus and Murdock, 1971). This is interpreted as due to the motivational effects of the subjects' evaluative concerns.

The interrelationship of role attitudes and performance cues should be noted. Often accompanying the arousal of a defensive role attitude is an increase in the subject's sensitivity to performance cues that he perceives will make him look good in the experiment. In two studies the responses the experimenter expected to obtain were made primarily by subjects whose evaluation apprehension had been aroused (Minor, 1970; Duncan, Rosenberg, and Finkelstein, 1969). The greater sensitivity of subjects with defensive role attitudes to performance cues that signal the hypothesis will lead to their more frequent confirmation of the experimenter's hypothesis.

The Negative Attitude.   Most subjects respond with either a cooperative or a defensive role attitude, but not all do so. Some attempt to ruin the experiment or at best behave in a fashion indicating that they will not cooperate with the experimenter and his scientific purposes. Although negativistic subjects have long been recognized, Masling (1966) emphasized their role in the experiment. He indelicately labeled the difficulty with these subjects as the "screw-you effect." It arises most commonly out of experimental situations with negative elements. Subjects may encounter an obnoxious experimenter who "turns them off," or the task may be excessively tedious or difficult. If the experiment is viewed as an interpersonal exchange much like a business deal, the costs for participation may so far exceed the rewards received from the experiment that the subject will respond to terminate the relationship as quickly as possible (Thibault and Kelley, 1959).

Some subjects may have negative attitudes before they enter the experiment. It has been suggested that these are most often found among subjects who are required by department or course regulations to participate in a certain number of psychology experiments (Cox and Sipprelle, 1971; Black, Schumpert, and Welch, 1972). They reluctantly appear in the experiment to emit routine behavioral data but have no real concern for their performance.

In the experiment the behavior of a subject with a negative attitude may take several forms. He may intentionally respond counter to what he perceives the experimenter desires and purposely ruin the experiment. Goldberg (1965) reported that although subjects were generally compliant, at least one made explicit her intention to ruin the study. She purposely chose the opposite of what the experimenter wanted because she did not like psychology or psychologists or their efforts to influence people. Experimental manipulations may also produce a generally negative response. This was demonstrated in an experiment (Silverman and Kleinman, 1967) that repeated with several modifications the classic study of displaced aggression (Miller and Bugelski, 1948). In the earlier study subjects who were frustrated negatively evaluated certain minority groups, presumably as evidence of their displaced aggression. In the more recent experiment subjects were given a variety of attitude measures in addition to the opportunity to displace their aggression to minority groups. The fact that subjects reacted negatively to *all* attitude measures, including those related to minorities, suggests that the frustration manipulation produced a general negativism.

In contrast to these obvious manifestations of role attitudes, negativism may be more subtly reflected in the routine, apathetic response of a subject who does not want to bother with confirming or rejecting the hypothesis. All he really cares about is ending the experiment as quickly as possible. This he can do most readily with minimum effort by complying with the experimenter's instructions as mechanically and efficiently as possible. Such behavior may often result in *apparently* "faithful" data. For example, subjects in verbal conditioning experiments who are aware of the experimenter's hypothesis yet who do not condition usually give the correct response at a chance level rather than reporting the desired response significantly less often.

Argyris (1968) suggests that negativistic subjects may even *cooperate* with the experimenter as the easiest way to fulfill their obligation. He proposed that by compelling subjects to participate in research in which they are never personally involved, we create a subject who behaves in a manner similar to the low-level employee in a large organization. The subjects demonstrate a number of contaminating behaviors typical of the employees' efforts to "beat the management." They show higher rates of absenteeism, cheating, and in general produce the minimum behavior that is acceptable. Most importantly, Argyris points out that failure to remedy the situation leads to research data that are at best extremely limited in their generalizability. The data may apply only to situations in which the interpersonal setting is similar to the peculiar relationship found between the experimenter and subject.

The Subject's Motivation: Concluding Remarks

Subjects should not be treated as inert objects for study. Not only is their awareness of the experiment's purposes a problem, but their attitudes, feelings, and motivations toward research must be considered. Indeed their knowledge of the hypothesis might be less of a problem if it were not for their desire to cooperate and to do well.

We do not fully understand the conditions under which the various role attitudes may be aroused. We are limited to a few general conclusions that may be derived from our survey. First, it is clear that subjects most often enter the experiment with a generally positive feeling that manifests itself in cooperation with whatever they are told to do, including confirmation of the hypothesis. Second, subjects are slightly apprehensive about how well they will perform. Whenever cues in the experiment make their apprehensive concerns salient, their behavior will be guided by a defensive attitude, even if they must disconfirm the experimenter's hypothesis. However, because looking good is frequently consistent with what the experimenter wanted, such subjects will often confirm the prediction. Finally, though subjects rarely approach the experiment with a negative attitude, role attitude cues in the experiment may arouse one. However, the precise form the negativistic behavior will take is unpredictable. It may be a purposeful disconfirmation of the hypothesis, a mechanical, apathetic response to the manipulations, or even simple confirmation of the hypothesis. Indeed, the dimensions of the negative role attitude are most unclear. Reviewing subject bias in the vast literature on attitude change, Silverman and Shulman (1970) conclude that many apparent inconsistencies in the research may be accounted for by differential role attitudes. Although their survey defines some of the conditions that lead to a specific motivation, the exact nature of the cues that will arouse one attitude or another remains unspecified.

Rather than defining these variables, one line of research has sought to examine experimental situations in which the various role attitudes may be competitively aroused. The aim of this research is to evaluate whether, for example, the cooperative or apprehensive role attitude will be adopted. This requires a situation in which to look good subjects will have to respond counter to the experimenter's hypothesis. In one study (Sigall, Aronson, and Van Hoose, 1970) it was proposed that if subjects were told that the experimenter expected the quantity of telephone numbers they copied to decrease, then looking good by copying more numbers would pit the two role attitudes against each other. Although support was found for the apprehensive role attitude in the larger quantity of numbers copied, a modified replication of the study (Adair and Schachter, 1972) suggests that the subjects actually perceived that the experimenter wanted the numbers to increase and that they had merely complied with what they thought was the hypothesis. In the latter study it was also proposed that rather than comparing role attitudes, a more profitable approach might be to search for the variables that elicit a cooperative or defensive response. Whether the subject confirms the hypothesis because he wishes to look good or to cooperate is relatively unimportant to more meaningful questions of what produces subject bias and what the investigator must do to correct it.

SUGGESTIONS FOR FURTHER READING

The Psychological Experiment

Riecken, H. W. 1962. A program for research on experiments in social psychology. In *Decisions, values and groups*, vol. 2, ed. N. F. Washburn, pp. 25–41. New York: Pergamon Press.

This analysis of the psychological experiment from the perspective of its participants is one of the classic papers that was the initial stimulus for research on the social psychology of the psychological experiment.

Subject Motivation

Silverman, I., and Shulman, A. D. 1970. A conceptual model of artifact in attitude change studies. *Sociometry* 33: 97–107.

The research on subject motivation in attitude change studies is reviewed and its impact assessed. It is concluded that although under most conditions subjects are motivated to cooperate with the experimenter, other motives may be aroused by conditions specific to the experiment.

Weber, S. J., and Cook, T. D. 1972. Subject effects in laboratory research: an examination of subject roles, demand characteristics, and valid inference. *Psychological bulletin* 77: 273–95.

In this comprehensive review of research on subject motivation, interpreted in a role theory framework, the authors find ample evidence for the apprehensive subject role in all experiments. Support for the cooperative, negativistic, and faithful roles is only indirect or lacking.

Demand Characteristics

Orne, M. T. 1962. On the social psychology of the psychological experiment: with particular reference to demand characteristics and their implications. *American psychologist* 17: 776–83.

In this classic paper Orne analyzes the experiment from the subjects' point of view. He proposes that subjects are responsive to the demand characteristics that signal the experimenter's hypothesis because of their problem-solving approach to the experiment and compliant attitudes.

Orne, M. T. 1970. Hypnosis, motivation and the ecological validity of the psychological experiment. In *Nebraska symposium on motivation,* ed. W. J. Arnold and M. M. Page, pp. 187–265. Lincoln, Neb.: University of Nebraska Press.

In this statement of demand characteristic theory Orne develops and extends his earlier views. After a review of the problems of motivation in hypnosis research, demand characteristics and quasi-controls are considered as they apply to experiments generally.

Evaluation Apprehension

Rosenberg, M. J. 1969. The conditions and consequences of evaluation apprehension. In *Artifact in behavioral research,* ed. R. Rosenthal and R. L. Rosnow, pp. 280–349. New York: Academic Press.

The development of the concept of evaluation apprehension is reviewed. Through a series of studies reported here the concept is supported and extended.

Sigall, H.; Aronson, E.; and Van Hoose, T. 1970. The cooperative subject: myth or reality? *Journal of experimental social psychology* 6: 1–10.

In a "crucial" study of subject motivation, the comparative strength of the apprehensive and cooperative roles were examined. In a situation in which subjects had to select between looking good and cooperating, the data support the former.

Adair, J. G., and Schachter, B. S. 1972. To cooperate or to look good? Subjects' and experimenters' perceptions of each other's intentions. *Journal of experimental social psychology* 8: 74–85.

This study challenges the conclusions of Sigall et al. Replication of portions of their study with detailed questioning of subjects suggest that the subjects may have been cooperating with what they perceived the experimenter desired rather than responding apprehensively to an evaluative threat.

Negativism

Argyris, C. 1968. Some unintended consequences of rigorous research. *Psychological bulletin* 70: 185–97.

This is the only systematic analysis of the source and form of negativistic subject behavior. From the perspective of organizational psychology the subject is viewed as possessing many of the motives and defenses of a low-level employee. The effect of this on behavior in the experiment is considered.

CHAPTER THREE

The Experimenter as a Demand Characteristic

Historically, psychological research has focused on the subject — his consciousness, behavior, and attitudes. The subject's responses have been observed, measured, and recorded and their individual differences taken into account in sampling procedures and studies of personality. The experimenter's attributes and individual differences and their contribution to the research process have generally been ignored.[1] The assumption has been that any experimenter could replicate the results of another study by duplicating procedures. For many years psychology has

> implicitly subscribed to the democratic notion that all *experimenters* are created equal; that they have been endowed by their graduate training with certain interchangeable properties; that among these properties are the anonymity and impersonality which allow them to elicit from the same subject identical data which they then identically observe and

[1] Periodically there have been exceptions to this lack of concern. Cason and Cason (1925) found that speed of reactions and number of unusual responses on a word association test varied as a function of the sex of both the experimenter and the subject. Although Barr (1932) found considerable agreement among results, he nevertheless examined the effect of different experimenters' employing the same technique in studies of sensory stimulation on learning. Postman and Jarrett (1952) found experimenter differences in their methods of administering reinforcements to subjects and concluded that, in situations involving the interaction of experimenter and subject, "We have paid too little attention to the contribution made by variations in E's behavior to the experimental results" (p. 253).

record. Just as inches were once supposed to adhere in tables regardless of the identity of the measuring instrument, so needs, motives, traits, IQs, anxieties, and attitudes were supposed to adhere to patients and subjects and to emerge uncontaminated by the identity and attitude of the examiner or experimenter [Friedman, 1967, pp. 3–4].

The impeccability of the experimenter has been dramatically challenged recently, and his contribution to the experiment as a prime source of artifact has become widely recognized (Rosenthal, 1966). Differences in the experimenter's personal characteristics such as his sex (Deutsch, Canavan, and Rubin, 1971; Montanelli and Hill, 1969; Harris, 1971), race (Sattler, 1970), and personality (level of test anxiety, for example; Winkel and Sarason, 1964) have been found to affect subjects' responses. Even the fact that the experimenter hypothesizes or expects certain results may alter his behavior toward subjects, to influence their responses to be consistent with his predictions (Rosenthal, 1966). Thus, in sharp contrast to our previous views of research, the experimenter may unintentionally affect his data in ways that seem unpredictable.

The influence of the experimenter arises from the subtle cues he unintentionally transmits to his subjects. From the subject's perspective, the experimenter's role as a demand characteristic is apparent. As the focal point of the experiment the subject looks to the experimenter as the key that will unlock the hidden purposes of the study. His instructions suggest how to respond, and his general appearance and conduct communicate other information about the experiment. Seemingly insignificant variations in the experimenter's mood, movement, or expression may seem to have special meaning and easily alter the subject's response. For example, a subject in a study of reaction time is, at the appointed time, met and brought into the laboratory by a somewhat harried-looking experimenter. He appears unable to stand still while he hurriedly reads the instructions and excitedly rummages through papers in preparation for the subject's first response. Understandably the subject feels uncomfortable and reacts to the nervousness of the experimenter, though his response is difficult to predict. He may be aroused to respond quickly and produce shorter latencies than he would have under normal conditions; on the other hand, the nervousness of the experimenter may be so distracting that the subject's reaction times are increased. Alternatively, the subject may become disturbed with his behavior, decide the entire study is as "nutty" as the experimenter, and refuse to cooperate, in which case his latencies will reflect his lowered motivation. Whether the experimenter serves as a performance cue or alters the subject's motivation toward the experiment, the reaction-time data will be biased — unintentionally and without knowledge of the experimenter. In all likelihood he was unaware of his nervousness and its potential effect on the subject's behavior. Nevertheless, these artifactual results have emerged from the cue value of his behavior as the significant demand characteristic in the experiment.

Systematic research into unintentional experimenter influence has been differentiated at the molar level into bias of two types: (1) direct influence by the experimenter on the subject's behavior, and (2) bias arising from errors in observing, recording, and interpreting data (Rosenthal, 1966). In the latter categories, it has been found that mathematical errors are generally biased toward the experimenter's hypothesis (Rosenthal, 1966). In other words, errors of addition or division in the computation of the mean usually systematically favor the hypothesis. These forms of bias, however, may be easily controlled by independent checks on computations or interpretations of data. Of greater concern is bias in which interactions with the subjects systematically alter their behavior to produce biased data. Such direct influence by the experimenter is also considered to be of two types — experimenter effects and expectancy effects (Rosenthal, Persinger, Vikan-Kline, and Mulry, 1963). This form of bias is so subtly produced that it may go undetected.

EXPERIMENTER EFFECTS

Experimenter effects include the biological, personal, or social attributes of the investigator that influence the subject to respond in a unique manner — unique in the sense that the subject would not have made the response if the experimenter had not possessed the critical attribute. Rosenthal (1967) has proposed three categories of experimenter effects: (1) *Bio-social effects* include bias resulting from any characteristic of the experimenter related to his bio-social identity, such as his sex, race, age, religion, physical appearance. (2) *Psycho-social effects* include influence arising from various personal traits and behaviors commonly measured by psychometric questionnaires, such as the experimenter's anxiety, hostility, authoritarianism, need for social approval. (3) *Situational effects* may be defined only in terms of specific experimenter-subject interactions or experimental situations, such as the effect of the warmth of the experimenter-subject relationship, the experimenter's relationship to the principal investigator, the appearance of the laboratory.

Variations in attributes or behaviors of the experimenter do not always lead to artifactual results (McGuigan, 1963). For example, brainstorming groups did not perform differently for experimenters who differed in age, sex, and relative status (Bouchard and Hare, 1970). Although it had been expected that the presence of a twenty-one-year-old female undergraduate experimenter would inhibit the frequency and free expression of novel responses by group members, relative to the output obtained by a thirty-year-old male professor, the dimensions on which they differed did not seem relevant to the production of novel ideas. Experimenters may systematically differ in ways that will not affect the data if none of the attributes is relevant to the particular response under investigation.

In other situations, the experimenter may influence the magnitude of the response of all subjects yet not affect treatment groups differentially. For example, a highly anxious experimenter may find generally more rapid verbal learning than that obtained by less anxious experimenters, but the rate and level of learning of subjects in different treatment groups — such as those given difficult versus those given easy lists to learn — may be unaffected by his behavior. Conclusions about learning difficult and easy material will be unaffected by these experimenter differences. Results from such studies would also be consistent with those of other studies, for the level of response of all subjects in both treatment groups would be uniformly affected.

Experimenter attributes or behavior become problematic, however, when they interact with the treatment conditions. In a study designed to test the hypothesis that pupil dilation could be used as a measure of heterosexual and homosexual interest, the relative response to photographs of male and female nudes varied as a function of the personal style of the experimenter (Chapman, Chapman, and Brelje, 1969). A "business-like graduate student" found no differences in reactions to the photographs; a "casual, outgoing undergraduate" experimenter found in his male subjects significantly greater pupil dilation to the female nudes. The behavior of the experimenter that led to a confirmation or disconfirmation of the hypothesis was specified; nevertheless, it is easy to see how different laboratories may obtain contrasting results. In a similar example, differential experimenter behavior led to variations in physiological responses not ordinarily under the subject's control and in the reported perception of neutral and taboo words. It was found that heart rate and sweating tended to decrease, and the time taken to report taboo words decreased with a sociable in contrast with either a reserved or an automated experimenter. Of particular interest were vasomotor changes reflecting support for a perceptual defense hypothesis among subjects tested by the automated experimenter but not with the reserved or sociable experimenter (Hicks, 1970). In yet another study the manner in which the

39

experimenter asked his subjects to extend a sixteen-hour fast to a twenty-four-hour fast significantly altered their plasma free fatty acid level as well as their perceived degree of hunger (Bogdonoff, Brehm, and Back, 1964). From these examples it is clear that variation in experimenter behavior is a potent, yet subtle, influence and that an interaction with treatments makes interpretation of results difficult, if not impossible.

Finally, it should be noted that interpersonal influence operates both ways. The subject's sex, age, warmth, or anxiety can elicit from the experimenter responses of attraction, anxiety, or hostility, which in turn may alter the subject's behavior. Presumably this has occurred in the consistent interaction of sex of subject and experimenter. In studies of serial learning of trigrams (Littig and Waddell, 1967), experimenter expectancy effects (Rosenthal, 1966), and the Rorschach Test (Harris and Masling, 1970), the performance of female subjects tested by male experimenters has been superior to that of any other subject-experimenter combination. Undoubtedly the presence of the opposite sex in the role of subject elicits from the male experimenter a special attention in the performance of his duties that in turn enhances the motivation or cues the performance of the female subject. This differential treatment was found in the greater number of sexual-romantic cards from the Thematic Apperception Test (TAT) male examiners presented to their female subjects (Masling and Harris, 1969). These "feedback loops" between the subject and examiner may also enhance the communication of the experimenter's expectancy (Rosenthal, 1967).

EXPERIMENTER EXPECTANCY EFFECTS

In addition to the effect of his personal attributes, the experimenter's expectations for certain results may lead him to behave in ways that unintentionally influence the subject's behavior. This could result in an artifactual confirmation of his hypothesis, as in the first study designed to demonstrate the expectancy effect (Rosenthal and Fode, 1963). Subjects were asked to rate a series of photographed faces on a scale ranging from $+10$ (extreme success) to -10 (extreme failure). One group of experimenters was led to expect that their subjects would average a $+5$ rating; the remaining experimenters expected a -5 rating, indicating perceived failure. Although the ratings were not as high or low as the experimenters' expectations, the difference between the two sets of ratings was significant. Subjects who the experimenter believed would rate the photographs as reflecting success indeed rated them more positively than subjects from whom the experimenter expected failure ratings. How did they do it? Was it mental telepathy? A rational explanation for expectancy effects can be found in the experimenters' behavior.

Communication of the Expectancy

Although he carefully designs an experiment so that his procedures are above reproach, the experimenter does not begin his study totally objective and naive. He expects to find differences between subjects, to get results consistent with the theory he is testing, and thus, often without conscious intent, he communicates to his subjects subtle performance cues consistent with his hypothesis. The subject, uncertain of the experiment's purpose, is attentive to experimenter-produced cues about how he should behave. Under optimum conditions the experimenter's expectancy is translated into the subject's hypothesis-confirming behavior.

The behaviors that are presumed to communicate the expectancy effect have been studied through a variety of techniques. Subjects' ratings of the experimenter's behavior (Rosenthal, Fode, Friedman, and Vikan-Kline, 1960), audio recordings of his voice (Duncan and Rosenthal, 1968), and video recordings of the total experimenter-subject interaction (Friedman, Kurland, and Rosenthal, 1965) have suggested that both kinesic (visual) and paralinguistic (verbal) cues from the experimenter may play a role. Although unable to specify the precise behaviors that communicate the expectancy, research has conclusively demonstrated that paralinguistic cues mediate bias effects (Adair and Epstein, 1968). In this study audio recordings of the instructions read by experimenters who expected and obtained biased results were used in place of a "live" experimenter in the person perception task already described. The tape-recorded voices of experimenters who had previously obtained bias were sufficient for reproducing the effects. In other words, the voice of the experimenter appeared to provide the appropriate performance cues.

This observation was confirmed subsequently by more sophisticated paralinguistic analyses by Duncan and Rosenthal (1968), who found that experimenters who were successful in obtaining bias gave a slight and presumably unintentional emphasis to the portion of the instruction that signaled their hypothesis. In a related study that confirmed these findings, Duncan, Rosenberg, and Finkelstein (1969) manipulated the experimenter's differential emphasis of the portion of the instructions that provided performance cues "slightly shaded" in the direction of positive or negative ratings of the photographs. They also found that the para-linguistic cues led to greater expectancy effects with increasing degrees of subject's evaluation apprehension. Apparently the subject with a defensive role attitude was sensitive to subtle cues from the experimenter, which he could then use to make himself look good.

It has also been suggested (Barber and Silver, 1968) that many instances of expectancy effects may be accounted for as recording or observing error rather than as a result of direct experimenter influence on the subject's behavior. The evidence from a word association study in which bias has been consistently obtained does not support this view (Johnson and Adair, 1970). By employing a tape-recorded monitor of the experimenter's presentation and the subject's responses to each word, it was possible to compare results observed and recorded by each experimenter with results independently recorded by an observer who was ignorant of the hypothesis. This comparison revealed that at least twice as much variance could be attributed to the direct influence of the experimenter's expectancy as to recording and observing errors. Thus, although we are unable to fully specify the cues that mediate the expectancy effect, it nevertheless appears that the experimenter, through some subtle transmission of performance and role attitude cues, may influence his subject to confirm his hypothesis.

The Extent of the Experimenter's Influence

The influence of the experimenter's expectancy has been demonstrated in such a variety of research contexts that it must be considered before undertaking any investigation. Although its effects have been most consistent in studies of animal learning,[2] it has been observed in more than fifty studies of reaction time, laboratory interviews, and inkblot tests as well as in the often-studied person perception task. Few areas of research appear to be immune from its influence.

In spite of this evidence, the pervasiveness and generality of the phenomenon have been challenged (Barber and Silver, 1968). It is contended that claims for the occurrence of bias have been made even when it has not been demonstrated and that there has been a failure to account for studies in which the effect has not been obtained. However, the effect has been observed so often that many failures to demonstrate it will be required before it may be considered a chance event. In addition, we

---

[2] Apparently it is relatively easy to communicate "encouragement" to "bright" rats and "discouragement" to "dull" rats by subtle differences in handling and in placing the animal in the apparatus (Rosenthal and Fode, 1963).

should keep in mind that the experimenter often needs to affect the behavior of only two or three subjects to alter a nonsignificant observation into a finding accepted at the 5 percent level of confidence. Thus, to deny existence of the expectancy effect or to suggest that its influence is weak is an ostrich-like stance that is not constructive (Page, 1971). If research findings may be altered or determined by an artifact such as the experimenter's expectancy, it is incumbent on the investigator to guard against it or to demonstrate that it has not influenced his data.

EXPECTANCY EFFECTS BEYOND THE LABORATORY

If the principles of social psychology are used to explain subject-experimenter interaction, then our developing understanding about the research process should in turn have application outside of the laboratory. This has certainly been true of the experimenter expectancy effect. The similarities of an experimenter's outcome expectation for his subjects and a teacher's expectations for the subsequent performance of a schoolchild are considerable. Research has dramatically shown that the teacher's positive expectations for the well-to-do child and negative bias toward the minority individual facilitate or impede the child's intellectual development (Rosenthal and Jacobson, 1968).

The expectations of the therapist or doctor for the outcome of an illness, drug treatment, or form of psychotherapy similarly influence their outcomes (Rosenthal, 1969b; Rosenthal and Frank, 1956; Goldstein, 1962). In many cases the outstanding early effectiveness of a treatment may be due to the great initial expectations for its success. The relative decline in documented effectiveness of disulfiram, a drug causing nausea and other unpleasant physiological reactions following consumption of alcohol, has been attributed to a decline in expectations since its enthusiastic introduction as a treatment for alcoholism (Lundwall and Baekeland, 1971).

The increased effectiveness of a specific treatment may be due as much to the subject's expectations as to the experimenter's expectancy. The subject who is to receive a treatment naturally expects to get better. In some cases it may not matter if he received the treatment or a placebo, an inert substance with no known therapeutic value. He would get better because he expects to. When the enthusiasm of the doctor or therapist who has high expectations for the treatment are added to this, optimum conditions for the treatment to show its healing capabilities exist. Thus, experimenter expectancy and placebo research in the laboratory have been extended to important roles in education and clinical practice.

SUGGESTIONS FOR FURTHER READING

Experimenter as a Demand Characteristic

McGuigan, F. J. 1963. The experimenter: a neglected stimulus object. *Psychological bulletin* 60: 421–28.

The author considers the problem of experimenter influence and concludes that we must make explicit attempts to generalize our results to a population of experimenters and accumulate some knowledge of the situations in which the experimenter may influence his subjects.

Rosenthal, R. 1966. *Experimenter effects in behavioral research*. New York: Appleton-Century-Crofts.

This classic survey of the effect of experimenter influence on research data is the most complete assessment of the problem. In addition to experimenter and expectancy effects, other forms of experimenter influence and ways of coping with this problem are discussed.

Effect of Experimenter's Race

Sattler, J. M. 1970. Racial "experimenter effects" in experimentation, testing, interviewing, and psychotherapy. *Psychological bulletin* 73: 137–60.

The author surveys in detail the effect of the race of the experimenter, the race of the subject, and their racial attitudes on research results. Effects are found with physiological responsiveness, test performance, personal preferences, and social desirability response bias.

Effect of Experimenter's Sex

Harris, S. 1971. Influence of subject and experimenter sex in psychological research. *Journal of consulting and clinical psychology* 37: 291–94.

A survey of recent journals reveals that the sex of the experimenter and of the subject is often ignored in the design of studies, though it can have a marked influence on results. Previous research documenting this influence in psychological testing and in studies of schizophrenia and sexual attitudes is reviewed.

Expectancy Effects

Rosenthal, R. 1969. Interpersonal expectations: effects of the experimenter's hypothesis. In *Artifact in behavioral research*, ed. R. Rosenthal and R. L. Rosnow, pp. 186–94. New York: Academic Press.

The author surveys and assesses research on expectancy effects. Examining areas of research in which the effect does not occur enables Rosenthal to draw conclusions about its generality and mode of transmission.

Duncan, S.; Rosenberg, M.; and Finkelstein, J. 1969. The paralanguage of experimenter bias. *Sociometry* 32: 107–219.

The role of paralinguistic cues in the transmission of expectancies is demonstrated in this study. Experimenters who signaled their hypothesis to subjects by purposely emphasizing key words in their instructions successfully obtained biased results.

The Controversy over the Generality of the Expectancy Effect

Barber, T. X., and Silver, M. J. 1968. Fact, fiction, and the experimenter bias effect. *Psychological bulletin monograph supplement* 70: 1–29.

Rosenthal, R. 1968. Experimenter expectancy and the reassuring nature of the null hypothesis decision procedure. *Psychological bulletin monograph supplement* 70: 30–47.

Barber, T. X., and Silver, M. J. 1968. Pitfalls in data analysis and interpretation: a reply to Rosenthal. *Psychological bulletin monograph supplement* 70: 48–62.

The existence, generality, and importance of expectancy effects are examined in this series of articles. In the first, Barber and Silver examine the available research and conclude that evidence for the phenomenon is lacking. In his reply, Rosenthal notes the large number of studies failing to demonstrate the effect that would be required to reject this concept. In the final paper Barber and Silver attempt to rebut this argument.

Expectancy Effects in the Classroom

Rosenthal, R., and Jacobson, L. 1968. *Pygmalion in the classroom.* New York: Holt, Rinehart and Winston.

This is a detailed report of the pioneering California school study in which teachers' expectations for their pupils' intellectual development were found to influence subsequent measures of intelligence. The implications of this research for education are discussed.

CHAPTER FOUR

Subject-Selection Bias and the Demand Characteristics of the Experiment

Ideally research is designed to ensure that the subjects are representative of the larger population to which the findings will be applied. If a phenomenon has been studied only with patients with a particular diagnosis, highly anxious subjects, or subjects with color vision deficiencies, then results are generalizable only to a corresponding population. This limitation is clearly recognized because the subjects have been purposely selected for their particular attribute or deficiency.

In most basic research the investigator wishes his subjects to be representative of the typical adult, and *random* selection of subjects is a common practice. By selecting every tenth family dwelling in a city or neighborhood, all students from one of several sections of an introductory psychology course, or all persons who sign up for a particular experiment as part of their research participation requirement,[1] it is presumed that no systematic differences in the attitudes or traits of subjects will emerge and that the samples will be representative of the general population. However, a truly random representative sample is difficult to obtain, and on occasion biased subject selection results.

---

[1] Self-selection is presumed to be random in the sense that subjects required to participate in a specific number of experiments will assign themselves to any given experiment without systematic bias. This assumption has been challenged by recent research to be discussed in this chapter.

SOURCES OF NONREPRESENTATIVENESS

Often bias occurs because selection procedures limit eligible subjects. Samples selected from telephone listings, automobile registrations, or the membership of civic clubs such as Rotary are biased in favor of persons of higher socio-economic status. The group on which an experiment is conducted may not appropriately represent the general population as the investigator had hoped. For example, although prison volunteers are often used for initial clinical drug trials, there is reason to believe that, because of their particular abnormal personality patterns, inmates may under-react to drugs. Although this was not found with inmates' reactions to the drug atropine (Weissman, Moore, Thomas, and Whitman, 1972), one must be cautious in assuming the appropriateness of prison populations for testing the effects of all drugs.

University Students

A major question about sampling representativeness concerns the appropriateness of university students as subjects on whom to base conclusions about the behavior of the general population. Because from 70 to 85 percent of published research (Smart, 1966; Schultz, 1969) and as much as 90 percent of research conducted by university psychology departments (Jung, 1969) use college subjects, this question cannot be ignored. Unfortunately, little direct evidence, aside from field experiments, verifies or rejects findings from university research, and the use of students remains relatively unchallenged. Nevertheless, if students behave differently from the general population, as the notion of the generation gap implies, for some research they cannot be considered as representative as we would like.

Added to this concern is the definite sex preference for subjects in psychological research. Approximately two-thirds of the subjects in published studies are male (Holmes and Jorgenson, 1971). This undoubtedly narrows further the applicability of research to the general population. In addition, only about one-third of the studies employed subjects of both sexes (Holmes and Jorgenson, 1971). It is true that some phenomena may be obtained only with male subjects — for example, the relationship of TAT measures of need for achievement and performance (McClelland, 1955) — and that others are peculiar to females — for example, the greater motivation of first-born children to be with others under conditions of stress (Schachter, 1959). The tendency to limit samples of subjects to one sex or the other, however, increases the chances of overlooking such important sex-related observations and may further limit the applicability of research findings.[2]

Each problem of sampling nonrepresentativeness may be readily accommodated in the investigator's procedures or interpretation of results. By employing an equal number of subjects of each sex, the experimenter may simultaneously examine his hypothesis and sex effects. If one sample is biased, an experimenter may seek another group of subjects on which to test his hypothesis, or he may acknowledge that his findings are limited to university students until the research has been conducted elsewhere. Potential biases in selection procedures should be carefully considered as part of the design of his study. In short, the experimenter has control over and should be able to exclude a large proportion of this form of subject bias.

Longitudinal Studies

Often certain forms of biased sampling are not under the investigator's control. Because of unsuspected changes in variables, biased sampling frequently occurs in studies of the same subjects over a period of time. Long-term studies examining intellectual and behavioral changes as a person ages (Rose, 1965; Riegel, Riegel, and Meyer, 1967) have found at each retesting that a smaller and less representative sample appears, the dropouts being due to illness, death, and other reasons. In one study it was found that the behavioral rigidity scores of those who were ill and of those who died were much greater than the initial scores for the subjects who appeared for the retesting (Riegel, Riegel, and Meyer, 1967). Similar extraneous reasons for subject loss have been found to bias studies of the effectiveness of treatments for alcoholism. Patients die, move from the city or otherwise become untraceable, or discontinue therapy for other nontreatment-related reasons (Miller, Pokorny, Valles, and Cleveland, 1970). In comparison with subjects who complete the treatment, the dropouts are often significantly different on a number of important variables and thus bias the sample. Nevertheless, the investigator in such cases could conclude that an experimental therapy was of little value if he did not find effects with a sample that was biased in his favor by a high dropout rate.

---

[2] Sex preference may increase the likelihood of negative results. It has been found that female subjects tested by male experimenters are more likely to confirm hypotheses than are male subjects tested by male experimenters (see Chapter 3).

SUBJECT-INITIATED SAMPLING BIAS

When subjects are permitted to choose the experiment in which they participate or when a portion of the sample is determined by their reactions to the research process itself, particularly difficult subject-selection problems arise. Self-selection is a common method of obtaining samples, and the differential willingness of subjects to volunteer or to complete a research-participation requirement often results in bias. Subjects who volunteer or keep their appointment for an experiment, for example, may differ from those who do not on a number of relevant variables. On the other hand, even though the subject volunteers, signs up, or otherwise agrees to participate in an experiment, his attitude toward the research may determine whether he is on time for his appointment and whether he will complete the experiment. Either of these reactions results in discarded data and a biased sample. With determination of the sample removed from the control of the investigator, correction of this form of bias becomes especially difficult.

Bias from Self-Selection

Whether a subject wishes to take part in an experiment should be a choice he is free to make. The need for his informed consent is one of the important ethical principles guiding human research. However, informed consent does not imply self-selection. Proper research procedures usually dictate that the investigator selects his own subjects in some predetermined random fashion and then obtains their consent to participate. The assumption that obtaining consent does not ordinarily disturb the randomness of the sample (because few decline) leads to further assumptions that erode careful sampling procedures. Some researchers ask, "Why can't I combine the consent and selection procedures? After all, the subject has to decide whether he will participate." Thus the prior consent of volunteers for an experiment is assumed and their participation obtained with little effort by the researcher. A somewhat similar line of reasoning is followed by psychologists who conduct their research with subjects from required-participation pools. However, to reduce their guilt for "coercing" subjects into experiments, these investigators maximize the subject's sense of freedom by permitting him to select from a number of alternatives. Thus one psychologist proudly proclaimed in his paper, "Participating in experiments was a course requirement, although students could choose freely from a large number of experiments." Underlying all self-selection procedures is the bold assumption that subjects will not choose the type or time of their participation, or decide whether they will participate at all, on the basis of some systematic bias. There is considerable recent research to suggest that this assumption is untenable.

Volunteers Versus Nonvolunteers. In spite of the fact that relatively few human subjects in university research are volunteers (only about 7 percent according to Jung, 1969), most studies on subject-selection bias have focused on the personality and attitudinal differences of these subjects from those who do not participate. To the extent that these differences are systematic, the volunteer sample will not be representative of the general population, which includes the nonvolunteer. The extensive research relevant to this question has been repeatedly reviewed, and the characteristics on which volunteers and nonvolunteers differ have been summarized (Rosenthal, 1965; Rosenthal and Rosnow, 1969; Rosnow and Rosenthal, 1970). Compared to nonvolunteers, volunteers were found to have a higher educational level and occupational status, need for social approval, and intelligence; they were lower in authoritarianism. With less confidence volunteers were found to be more sociable, arousal-seeking, conventional, younger, and more often first-born than were nonvolunteers. In addition women tended to volunteer more than men for routine tasks; with unusual tasks the sex difference was reversed. Thus a set of fairly stable, distinguishing characteristics can be attributed to volunteers.

The different attributes of volunteers and nonvolunteers do not produce biased results. The differences must be relevant to the behavior under investigation. If volunteers are less authoritarian and authoritarians are more prejudiced, then evidence of prejudice and discrimination in a study restricted to volunteer subjects will be systematically underestimated. It is particularly disturbing when differences interact with the demand characteristics or treatments. For example, volunteers' greater need for social approval presumably leads them to be more concerned about either helping the experimenter to validate his hypothesis or performing in such a fashion as to look good to the experimenter and thus winning his favorable evaluation. Thus, if the demand characteristics of the experiment facilitate their predisposition toward a cooperative role attitude and an awareness of a hypothesis that is consistent with the experimenter's prediction, volunteers will show greater cooperation with the experimenter than will a less biased sample. This happened in a study of attitude change (Rosnow and Rosenthal, 1966) in which an investigator who was judged to have moderate anti-fraternity views presented a one-sided communication on fraternities to volunteer and nonvolunteer subjects. To half of the subjects in each group, the communication was negative toward fraternities; to the other half, the investigator presented a positive communication. The results were consistent with the volunteer subjects' greater need for approval and greater tendency to cooperate with the experimenter. Volunteers agreed with what they perceived to be the experimenter's anti-fraternity attitudes; the nonvolunteers responded more in favor of the pro-fraternity communication. The subject-selection procedure in this study led to different results, contingent upon the subject's perception of and reaction to the performance and role attitude cues in the experiment.

Certain experiments attract particular types of subjects, thus creating another form of volunteer bias. For example, the first child born into a family, primarily because of his interactions with his parents, has a desire to be with others under certain conditions. This affiliative tendency extends to their participation in research. When freshman university students were solicited for a small group experiment, a greater proportion of first-borns than later-borns volunteered for the study (Capra and Dittes, 1962). This sampling bias further contaminates research to the extent that other differences associated with birth order may systematically influence the subjects' responses to the treatments and demand characteristics in the group experiment.

Compulsory Subject Pools.   The widely acknowledged problems of bias with volunteers and the convenience of a ready source of subjects have led many departments of psychology to construct pools of "coerced" subjects from undergraduate students. To require that all students participate ensures that subjects who would otherwise be nonvolunteers are included in a sample. This objective is defeated, however, by investigators who allow their subjects to select the time and experiment to fulfill their requirement. Many of the problems associated with self-selected volunteer samples emerge in different form. For example, the attitudes toward hypnosis of coerced subjects who "volunteered" for a hypnosis experiment were found to be significantly more positive than were those of coerced subjects who volunteered for other types of studies (Melei and Hilgard, 1964).

The volunteer-nonvolunteer bias also emerges in the form of a beginning-of-the-term willing subject versus an end-of-the-term reluctant participant. Subjects who selected to participate at various times during the year have been found to differ in their attitudes toward psychological research (Adair, 1970*b*). End-of-the-year subjects had significantly less positive attitudes toward research than did subjects who chose to participate earlier. To the extent that attitudes influence response to the experiment, these differences may be translated into biased samples (Adair and Fenton, 1971). This systematic overrepresentation of certain types of subjects in samples drawn at different times of the term suggests a potential nonrepresentativeness in all sampling by self-selection from compulsory subject pools.

Bias from Subject's Reactions to Research

Even though subjects have been carefully selected and all appear for the experiment on time, sampling problems may arise in response to the research itself. The manner in which subjects have been treated, their perception of the experimental situation and manipulations, or their research experience just prior to the study may systematically alter their attitudes and performance and in the extreme case may cause some to discontinue participation.

"Dropouts."   Although subjects in studies that involve only a single session generally do not refuse to complete an experiment once they have begun, it is not uncommon in a large study for three or four subjects to discontinue their participation. On closer examination of the experiment they have found that what they are asked to disclose or the experimental manipulation is more than they care to reveal or experience. The similarity of these few subjects to those who previously opted out through a self-selection recruitment process suggests a cumulative sampling bias that is difficult to assess or control.

In longitudinal studies — long-term studies of the same subjects — or experiments lasting for more than one session, the dropout rate is a major sampling concern. In the alcohol treatment research (Miller, Pokorny, Valles, and Cleveland, 1970) mentioned earlier, more than one-fourth of the patients failed to complete therapy in addition to the number who moved away or died. Some may have dropped out for reasons unrelated to the treatment program, but it is likely that many reacted against the procedures, felt it was a waste of time, did not like the therapist, and found the required, active group participation unpleasant. Comparison of profiles revealed that those who dropped out were significantly more "sick" than those who completed the program. Similarly, reactions toward the research were found to influence results in longitudinal studies of aging (Riegel, Riegel, and Meyer, 1967) and in a follow-up study of the effectiveness of a child guidance clinic program (Speer and Zold, 1971).

Although the investigator is at the mercy of his dropouts, one should not conclude that the limited sample of subjects who remain is not worth studying. Indeed such research may reveal that a particular type of patient prefers a particular treatment or that a treatment is at least effective with a sample biased in its favor. If a treatment is found to be ineffective with a biased sample, it is unlikely that it will be successful with an even more representative sample. By examining and reporting dropout rates and modifying interpretations accordingly, self-selection though noncompletion of an experiment may be monitored and its influence understood.

Prior Experimental History. Another potential sampling bias may arise from the subjects' reaction to prior research. It is difficult for an investigator to control the immediately preceding experiences of his sample and a sizable number of subjects with a uniform research history may contaminate results. It has been found that consistent positive or negative research histories (Holmes and Appelbaum, 1970) and participation in studies that involve deception (Weber and Cook, 1972) may influence subsequent performance. The fact that some research has not been affected by previous deceptions suggests that the form of the deceit and of the subsequent research may be important.

The extensive participation of each individual, as required in compulsory subject pools, undoubtedly biases the performance of experienced subjects. Indeed, the multi-experiment requirement probably serves as a training program for perceiving and responding to demand characteristics. With practice the subject acquires insights into the psychologist's procedures and methods and becomes better able to discern the relevant performance and role attitude cues. As a result, sophisticated subjects, defined by amount of research experience, time of participation, or level of training in psychology, have been found more often to be aware of the hypothesis and to cooperate more than naive subjects. This has been observed in studies of verbal operant and classical conditioning (Holmes, 1967; Page, 1969), attitude change (Silverman, 1968*a*), and figure-ground perception (Page, 1968). Thus samples in which sophisticated subjects predominate because of the time of year or another peculiarity of the selection process will favor confirmation of the experimenter's hypothesis.[3]

[3] Two processes may be operating. On the one hand, positive attitudes toward research found in samples early in the year may reflect a self-selection process; that is, as a whole, positive-attitude subjects tend to complete their participation requirement early (Adair, 1970*b*). At the same time, an individual's attitudes toward research may become more positive and his knowledge of research becomes greater as he gains research experience.

Bias from Compulsory Participation in Research

Students' reactions to required participation in research are another potential source of bias. To the extent that they feel coerced or unfairly used, laboratory subjects may become poorly motivated or negativistic. For example, in an attitude change study a "boomerang" effect — an opinion counter to the advocated position — was obtained from subjects who had no choice about participating (Holmes and Strickland, 1970). The negative attitude change was attributed to the subject's retaliation for being forced to participate.

Evidence suggests that coerced subjects are poorly motivated. Comparison of pursuit rotor performance revealed that volunteers had a greater accuracy and perseverance than did coerced subjects (Black, Schumpert, and Welch, 1972). The partial reinforcement extinction effect was also found to occur only with volunteers. In other words, intermittent rather than consistent reinforcement (in the form of knowledge of results) led volunteers to persevere on the pursuit rotor whereas this variable had no differential effect on coerced participants. Interaction of the treatment with the sample variable raises serious questions about selection procedures. A similar failure to obtain an experimental result with coerced subjects that had been obtained previously with volunteers — namely, operant conditioning of acceleration and deceleration of heart rate — was also attributed to their lowered motivation and apathetic response (Cox and Sipprelle, 1971).

Unfortunately, in both studies it is difficult to determine whether the poorer performance of coerced subjects reflected their lowered motivation or whether the volunteer samples did not include the nonvolunteers found in compulsory subject pools. It is also possible that volunteers came from an entirely different pool of potential subjects and responded to an appeal different from those of coerced subjects. Although it is not clear whether the apparent lowered motivation of coerced subjects is due to their lack of freedom to decide their participation, differences between volunteers and coerced samples must be resolved. However, we should be cautious in interpreting failure to find with coerced subjects effects that have been demonstrated with volunteers as an indication that one sampling procedure is more valid than another (Adair, 1972b). Unfortunately, so little research has been devoted to the effects of coercion and the ecological validity of common sampling procedures that it is not possible at this time to condemn or favor one selection method or another.

CONCLUSION

Subject selection is a triadic interaction of investigator, study, and subject. Just as in the laboratory experiment, the attitudes and thoughts of the subject toward the research, the experimenter's approach to his sample, and the type of study and the subjects' part in it combine to confuse the process. The population from which the experimenter solicits his subjects and his manner of selection cannot be taken lightly. The potential for bias may be found in the experiment itself — in the task and instructions and in the subject's approach to the study. The investigator should not introduce further bias by his selection of subjects. If the experimenter is aware of the subtle forms of sampling bias, is sensitive to its potential in his study, and makes his own selection of subjects or studies the effect of other procedures when he cannot, he will have taken the necessary precautions.

SUGGESTIONS FOR FURTHER READING

Sampling Practices

Smart, R. 1966. Subject selection bias in psychological research. *Canadian psychologist* 7: 115–21.

Jung, J. 1969. Current practices and problems in use of college students for psychological research. *Canadian psychologist* 10: 280–90.

Schultz, D. P. 1969. The human subject in psychological research. *Psychological bulletin* 72: 214–28.

The sampling practices of psychologists were surveyed in each of these studies. Smart and Schultz counted the frequency of various sampling practices reported in selected social and experimental journals. Jung reports a mail survey of human subject sampling practices in departments of psychology in North America. Their general conclusions are similar: Psychologists overuse college stu-

dents, largely through compulsory subject pools established in psychology departments.

King, D. J. 1970. The subject pool. *American psychologist* 25: 1179–81.

Consideration is given to the pool of introductory psychology subjects — why it was needed, what problems it created, and how they were handled by one psychology department.

Volunteers Versus Nonvolunteers

Rosenthal, R., and Rosnow, R. L. 1969. The volunteer subject. In *Artifact in behavioral research,* ed. R. Rosenthal and R. L. Rosnow, pp. 59–118. New York: Academic Press.

Rosnow, R. L., and Rosenthal, R. 1970. Volunteer effects in behavioral research. *New directions in psychology,* vol. 4, pp. 213–77. New York: Holt, Rinehart and Winston.

The authors survey the research on sampling bias arising from the use of volunteer subjects. In addition to assessing the traits and attiudes that differentiate the volunteer from the nonvolunteer, research on their differential reactions to the laboratory experiment is considered.

Sex Bias

Holmes, D. S., and Jorgenson, B. W. 1971. Do personality and social psychologists study men more than women? *Representative research in social psychology* 2: 71–76.

This is a survey of sex preferences in human subject sampling in personality and social psychological research. In three selected journals, preference for male subjects over females was even greater than the preference for college student subjects over noncollege subjects.

Order-of-Appearance Bias

Cope, C. S., and Kunce, J. T. 1971. Unobtrusive behavior and research methodology. *Journal of counseling psychology* 18: 592–94.

The relative order in which subjects appeared for an experiment was related to their linguistic behavior in the laboratory group sessions.

Bias from Prior Experiments

Holmes, D. S., and Appelbaum, A. S. 1970. Nature of prior experimental experience as a determinant of performance in a subsequent experiment. *Journal of personality and social psychology* 14: 195–202.

Subjects whose prior experimental history had been "dull and a waste of time" were compared with those who had been led to find research "interesting and important" and are found to be significantly inferior in conscientiousness, problem-solving, cooperative behavior intentions, and in actual performance in a subsequent test experiment.

CHAPTER FIVE

Measurement and Control
of Social Artifacts:
Experimenter Bias

In response to the social artifacts described in preceding chapters, techniques have been developed to assess the extent to which data may have been contaminated by the experimenter's expectancy or by the subject's awareness of the hypothesis. These procedures are similar to the control groups used to assess the effect of the independent variables on the subject's behavior. In this traditional approach, control subjects are presented with conditions virtually identical to those of the experimental group, the only exception being the experimental treatment. Differences between data from the two sets of subjects may then be attributed to their differential exposure to the treatment variable.

Analogously, the impact of the experimenter's expectancy may be assessed by comparing the effects of the instructions and treatments presented by the experimenter who hypothesizes certain results with the data collected by an experimenter with an opposite bias (Rosenthal, 1966). The possibility that subjects' behavior may merely reflect what they perceived the investigator wanted may similarly be determined by comparisons of data from experimental and specially treated control subjects. These subjects are called "quasi-controls" (Orne, 1969), for in contrast to traditional controls the subject *actively* assists the experimenter to understand the social contaminants of the study.

With the knowledge gained from these techniques the investigator may adjust his procedures to obviate these effects or take them into account in his interpretation of the data. In this chapter controls for measuring the effects of the experimenter's expectancy and techniques for preventing its influence are considered. In the next chapter quasi-controls for measuring the effect of the subject's awareness will be examined.

EXPERIMENTER EXPECTANCY CONTROL GROUPS

Consider an investigator in the area of verbal learning who has predicted that anxiety-arousing instructions will enhance performance. He designs a study to test this hypothesis. One group of subjects will receive ego-involving instructions that arouse their anxiety, and the others will receive the standard task-oriented presentation. Although a comparison of the two groups may reveal the predicted effect of the investigator's manipulations, the contribution of the experimenter's expectancy to this result is not clear. The subject may be sensitive to the exact manner in which the research assistant, who shares the investigator's expectations, presents the instructions. Thus the investigator will need some indication of the effect of both expectations and instructions.

To separate and obtain a measure of the expectancy effect he will need to add a couple control groups. Just as he had designed his study to compare the experimental and standard instructions, he will want to compare data collected by the experimenter who expects one result with data obtained under the opposite expectation. Because the research assistant already has expectations for anxiety-arousing and neutral instructions, the investigator will need only to reverse these expectations for the two control groups. This could be accomplished by falsely telling the assistant that subjects in the extra two groups have been selected for their scores on the Taylor Manifest Anxiety Scale and that the high-anxious subjects will show improved performance under the neutral instructions they will receive. Ostensibly the low-anxious subjects simply cannot be aroused to greater performance by the ego-involving instructions. Thus their relative performance may be expected to be the opposite of that of the experimental subjects.

Unfortunately, this control technique depends on the successful deception of a fairly sophisticated experimenter. If he does not believe the opposing expectancies, the interpretation that may be placed upon the control group data is limited. However, effective procedures for inducing expectancies are at the investigator's disposal (Rosenthal, 1966). In addition to ascribing certain traits or characteristics to subjects, other "special" conditions in the expectancy control groups — such as prior experimental histories or treatments — may ostensibly reverse the expected treatment effects. With more than one experimenter the options for inducing expectancies are increased. For example, if one experimenter presented the instructions and another collected the data, the labels for the treatment groups could be reversed for the data-collecting experimenter so that he expected treatment effects from control subjects and vice versa. Alternatively, the investigator may disparage the strength of the treatment to the control experimenter so that he expects it to have no effect, or he may reverse the theory presented to him so that opposite results are anticipated.

Assuming these induced expectations have been effective, the investigator would merely compare the performance of the expectancy controls with his original groups to assess the effect of the expectancy on his results. If, in the extreme case, he found good or poor verbal learning *only* from groups the experimenters *expected* to perform well or poorly, the effect of the instructions independent of expectancies would be negligible. On the other hand if verbal learning performance varied only according to whether the subject had received the anxiety-arousing instructions, the hypothesis would have been supported. Of course, results somewhere in between could have been obtained. The experimenter's expectation may have influenced subjects who received neutral instructions, and the anxiety-arousing instructions may have led to superior performance regardless of the results the experimenter expected. In any event the interpretation would become more definitive as the investigator excludes or takes into account as a social contaminant the experimenter's expectancy.

Although expectancy controls appear to require a large number of additional subjects and experimenters, an extravagant expansion of the study is not required (Rosenthal, 1966). One experimenter induced with differential expectancies by one of the methods just suggested could presumably test all four groups of subjects. In addition, by using half of the usual number of subjects in each group and by using the other half of the subjects in the expectancy control groups, the investigator may be able to simultaneously test his hypothesis and for expectancy effects without increasing the size of the sample. If the expectancy effect is found to be negligible, the control subjects, differing from the real subjects only in the experimenter's expectancy, may then be combined with the real subjects in the test of the hypothesis. Further economy is realized if it is demonstrated that a given area of research is free of expectancy effects. Clearly, then, the use of expectancy control groups is an inexpensive investment that can at least provide knowledge of this source of socially based contamination of research.

TECHNIQUES FOR PREVENTING
EXPERIMENTER EXPECTANCY EFFECTS

Since unintentional influence is based on the subtle performance and role attitude cues the experimenter provides the subject, an investigator may prevent expectancy effects by removing the experimenter or minimizing his contact with the subject. This could be accomplished by automating the presentation of instructions, the collection of data, or the entire experiment, or by keeping the experimenter ignorant of the treatment conditions and thus ignorant of the appropriate cues to transmit. Each of these techniques is effective.

Automation of the Experiment

Because the greatest potential for the transmission of bias exists in the presentation of instructions, this part of the experiment has most often been automated. Written, tape-recorded, filmed, or televised instructions minimize the interaction of the experimenter and subject (Rosenthal, 1966). Tape-recorded instructions are frequently used and have been found to reduce expectancy effects at least among male experimenters (Johnson and Adair, 1972). If they are prepared prior to the experiment and without knowledge of the treatment conditions, the opportunity for transmitting bias will be greatly reduced. The effects that do emerge will be distributed randomly with no opportunity for direct experimenter influence from instruction-reading behavior. Moreover, automated instructions save wear and tear on experimenters who would show fatigue or boredom from having to read the same instructions many times during a lengthy study.

It is equally important to control for bias in the collection of the data. For example, in one study (Johnson and Adair, 1972) female experimenters showed greater expectancy effects under automated instructions, presumably because of observing and recording errors rather than because of any communicated expectancy. By requiring the subject to record his own responses (Adair and Epstein, 1968) or by automated data collection with electronic timers or counters (Johnson, 1970), intentional or unintentional biasing of the data as they are recorded can be prevented.

Finally, total replacement of the experimenter by a computer is not only possible but has been demonstrated (Videbeck and Bates, 1966;

Johnson, 1967). Videbeck and Bates "verbally conditioned" the subjects' use of certain pronouns by programming a computer to type the word "good" as a reinforcement whenever the subject responded appropriately. They found the same differential conditioning of aware and unaware subjects that has been found so often in this research and concluded that a computer-run experiment yielded results comparable to those obtained with the traditional procedure.

In a similar study Johnson (1967) converted an IBM 1620 computer into an automated experimenter to administer an entire problem-solving study including the selection of stimulus materials for each trial. Without the interaction of subject and experimenter, of course, problems of experimenter influence were resolved. Reporting only preliminary findings, Johnson suggests that although mean problem solution is similar whether the data are collected by an experimenter or by a computer, performance with the computer is much less variable. This reduction of error variance enables the investigator to make more powerful tests of his hypotheses.

There are, however, disadvantages to automation by computer. For some time the costs of computer hardware and of extensive programming for human response contingencies will be great. Thus few investigators will be able to afford to use a computer as an automated solution to expectancy effects. In addition, subjects' peculiar responses to interaction with a machine are yet to be explored. There is a suggestion that their reactions may be different from responses to humans (Schwitzgebel and Traugott, 1968).

The "Blind" Experimenter

In view of the costs and limited availablity of computers, interactions of subjects, experimenters, and data collectors without anyone's knowledge of the hypothesis or particular treatment being tested may afford a more practical protection from expectancy effects. An excellent study designed to test the hypothesis that people like those who punish their enemies and reward their friends (Aronson and Cope, 1968) illustrates how "blind" experimenter–subject contact limits expectancy effects in a study involving considerable interaction. To begin the study the experimenter, ignorant of the treatments to follow, read rather extensive instructions to each subject. After the instructions, the treatment to be administered to the subject was determined, and the experimenter responded in a pleasant or harsh manner to the subject's creative stories. Immediately following this manipulation the supervisor, ignorant of whether the subject had been treated harshly or pleasantly, appeared in the research room and acted harshly or pleasantly toward the experimenter. The experimenter, during his treatment of the subject, did not know whether the supervisor was about to treat him harshly or pleasantly. Finally, the departmental secretary collected the dependent variable — that is, whether the subjects would volunteer to assist the supervisor — but she was ignorant of the subject's condition with respect to both the supervisor's treatment of the experimenter and the experimenter's treatment of the subject. Thus a complex design involving the interaction of the subject with three investigators was conducted with blind controls throughout. Such careful procedures certainly reduce the possibility of expectancy effects.

Occasionally, however, it is difficult to maintain the experimenter's "blindness." For example, in a comparison of the symptoms of mental illness of normal, obese, and hyperobese women (Holland, Masling, and Copley, 1970), it was impossible to keep the interviewer blind to the size of his subject. Blind controls in a study using subjects with positive and negative attitudes toward psychological research were similarly ineffective (Adair, 1970*b*). In this instance the behavior of the first few subjects revealed the groups to which they belonged and removed the experimenter's blindness for the remaining subjects in these groups. In situations in which guarding against the experimenter's expectancy is impossible, control groups designed to measure its effect are essential for an adequate interpretation of the data. Nonetheless, in many situations blind experimentation should be effective.

Additional Procedures

Other techniques are available to prevent or reduce expectancy effects (Rosenthal, 1966). Increasing the number of experimenters may be helpful. Larger numbers of experimenters increase the generality of results and randomize expectancies. Because each tests fewer subjects, it would be easier to maintain blindness and to decrease the probability of an experimenter's learning influence techniques. A more radical approach would be to employ professional psychological experimenters who would presumably have less ego-involvement in collecting data in accord with their expectations (Rosenthal, 1966). Such experimenters would be carefully selected and would receive greater pay and training for their services; thus it would also be possible to utilize maximum controls for expectancy effects.

THE NECESSITY OF EXPECTANCY CONTROLS

Assessing the influence of the experimenter's expectancy and designing procedures that prevent or reduce its effect is an involved process, made less appealing by the knowledge that not all research is susceptible to such contamination. Economy of effort could be achieved if controls were found to be necessary in only certain areas of research. Unfortunately, expectancy research has not yet revealed the areas. There is a possibility that ambiguous stimuli or tasks — inkblot testing (Masling, 1965; Marwit and Marcia, 1967) — and tasks that involve considerable experimenter-subject interaction — laboratory interviews (Rosenthal, 1969a) — are more susceptible to bias effects. On the other hand, psychophysical judgments (Shames and Adair, 1967) that restrict the range of the subjects' responses appear to be less susceptible. Because of limited expectancy research, however, these conclusions must be considered tentative.

In another sense, the need for expectancy controls is clear. By initially employing them, the investigator may define for himself whether his research is susceptible to bias, and, at the same time, add to the general knowledge of when controls are necessary. It may be that much research, indeed most, is not susceptible to the influence of experimenter expectancy. Nevertheless, its effect in only one study may have unfortunate consequences for the investigator who is led astray. Certainly the minimal effort required to avoid expectancy effects and to measure their presence is warranted to ensure that the research is devoid of contamination by the experimenter as a demand characteristic.

MEASUREMENT AND CONTROL OF EXPERIMENTER EFFECTS

The influence on research data of the experimenter's sex, anxiety, and other personal characteristics is much more difficult to control and measure. It is especially difficult to detect because the attribute that leads to artifactual results may not be apparent and therefore cannot be studied by intentional manipulation. Added to this is the common practice of using only one experimenter in a study, thus removing the opportunity for comparisons. These problems argue for the obvious solution: Some form of experimenter sampling is just as necessary as subject sampling for an adequate test of a hypothesis. No longer can psychology afford to concentrate exclusively on the subject and his behavior and ignore the experimenter. The experimenter is half of this social interaction, and his contribution to the data must be assessed or controlled.

SUGGESTIONS FOR FURTHER READING

Expectancy Controls

Rosenthal, R. 1966. *Experimenter effects in behavioral research.* New York: Appleton-Century-Crofts.

The last section of Rosenthal's text (pp. 331–413) is a detailed treatment of methods for control of experimenter expectancy effects. In six chapters he successively considers experimenter sampling, experimenter behavior, personnel considerations, blind and minimized contact, and expectancy control groups as proposed solutions to the problem of expectancy effect.

The Computer as Experimenter

Videbeck, R., and Bates, H. D. 1966. Verbal conditioning by a simulated experimenter. *Psychological record* 16: 145–52.

This computer-run verbal conditioning study replicates the previous findings of conditioning effects with aware subjects only and illustrates the use of the computer in the experiment.

The Blind Experimenter

Aronson, E., and Cope, V. 1968. My enemy's enemy is my friend. *Journal of personality and social psychology* 8: 8–12.

Control of expectancy effects by keeping the experimenter ignorant of the treatments the subject has received and will subsequently experience is effectively illustrated by this study.

CHAPTER SIX

Quasi-Control Procedures to Assess Subject Bias

After the study is over, the data are in, and the hypothesis confirmed, a nagging question remains: Was it confirmed merely because the subjects cooperated and gave the investigator the data he wanted? "How do I know?" he might well ask. "I manipulated certain variables, controlled others, and obtained results consistent with my prediction. That's good enough for me. After all, how do I know the subjects' thoughts or what they responded to?" This is the most important question in psychological research. There is not an easy answer to it.

Because of the qualities of the human subject and his interaction with the experimental situation, subject bias is a potential problem in any study. Ignoring it will not make it disappear. Conclusive interpretation of data is difficult, if not impossible, when subjects' perceptions of the experimental situation, awareness of the hypothesis, and adoption of common role attitudes influence their responses. In some way the investigator must sort out the portion of the subjects' behavior attributable to the experimental treatment from the portion due to these social artifacts.

To do so requires an understanding of the subjects' perceptions, motivations, and intentions within the experiment. For the most part, these are private events, and the investigator is privy to them only with the consent of his subject. Thus he must solicit the subjects' assistance in specifying the performance and role attitude cues that have governed their behavior. Because these cues often are not readily apparent, three special quasi-control procedures (Orne, 1969) have been developed — the post-experiment inquiry, the nonexperiment, and simulating subjects.

POST-EXPERIMENT INQUIRY

The greatest source of information about the subject's awareness is his own verbal report. Often at the end of the experiment the subject is asked to indicate the most salient features of the study and to recall how he viewed them. This inquiry may occur as a casual conversation between the experimenter and subject, or it may consist of structured questions in an interview or written questionnaire. The more formal inquiry, of course, yields more reliable data, which may be subsequently verified or rejected.

The written questionnaire has been effectively used by Page (1968, 1969, 1970; Page and Scheidt, 1971). He has employed it to document the influence of subjects' awareness and common role attitudes on the conditioning of affective meaning. In the original conditioning study (Staats and Staats, 1958) it had been concluded that repeated pairing of nonsense syllables with positively or negatively toned adjectives such as "good" and "dirty" had altered the affective meaning of these previously neutral syllables. Presumably this was to have occurred through conditioning of which the subjects were unaware. In Page's study careful use of the written post-experiment questionnaire revealed a number of subjects who "conditioned" because they were aware of the hypothesis and had cooperated (Page, 1969). Thus the post-experiment inquiry documented the possible influence of demand characteristics and the need for a more sophisticated research design to conclusively demonstrate the conditioning interpretation independent of these artifacts.

The post-experiment inquiry is one of the most difficult quasi-control techniques to employ. The wording of the questions, their ordering, and presentation to the subject are delicate matters that must be given thought and pilot testing or trial runs. For example, Page's seventeen-item questionnaire had to be carefully constructed. Initially several broad questions were used to explore the subjects' general awareness of the experiment's purpose. Toward the conclusion of the inquiry the level or degree of awareness was assessed by more specific questions about crucial experimental procedures. The transition from the general to the specific avoided cueing the subject early in the questionnaire about the kinds of answers the experimenter desired and yet tapped the minimal awareness that may have influenced behavior. Moreover, the placing of each item on a separate page insured that "awareness" was not affected by "guidance" from the later, more detailed portion of the questionnaire. In spite of these precautions Page was criticized (Staats, 1969) for providing the subject with obvious performance cues in the inquiry portion of the experiment and hence disclosing an excess of pseudo-aware subjects. Although we attempt to avoid cueing subjects, it is difficult to specify the demand characteristics that govern the inquiry. Too many leading questions may suggest to the subject that the experimenter really wants him to be aware or will think he is stupid if he does not give the correct hypothesis. This may be further complicated by the perception that the role attitude that governed the subject's behavior in the experiment is to continue during the post-experiment inquiry. In other words, the subject may be motivated by his desire to look good or to please the experimenter on the questionnaire just as he was during the experiment.

Alternatively, if the subject perceives that to respond with the correct hypothesis would invalidate the research and his previous experiment behavior, he may well withhold the information the investigator needs (Orne, 1962). This "pact of ignorance" has been empirically demonstrated (Levy, 1967). Subjects who were incidentally told the verbal conditioning hypothesis by a confederate and behaved in accord with this information nevertheless failed to reveal their awareness on a post-experiment questionnaire. A fine balance of thoroughly querying the subject without revealing to him the desired answers must be achieved.

These cautions in the interpretation of data from the post-experiment inquiry stem from our lack of knowledge of the technique. Although it has been extensively used, there has been little uniformity in questioning procedures. Furthermore, there has not been any systematic effort to design the technique to meet the specific demands of the quasi-control problem. What is needed is basic research on the optimum forms of questioning to obtain the maximum valid information and to specify the areas of research where the technique is most applicable.

Nevertheless, advances in the contemporary acceptance of the post-experiment inquiry as a quasi-control have revived the use of the subject's uniquely human characteristics of awareness and verbal report as an aid to understanding experiment behavior. No longer is the investigator dependent exclusively on the subjects' selective recall and report, as in psychology's distant past, or on the almost exclusive concern with the effect of manipulations on motor movements and overt behavior. He is free to explicitly utilize queries about the subject's awareness as an adjunct or supplemental research method.

THE NONEXPERIMENT

In the nonexperiment a special group of quasi-control subjects selected from the population from which the experimental group was drawn are instructed to imagine themselves as subjects in an experiment that is described to them. After exposure to all the details — the experimenter, the apparatus, and an explanation of the study equivalent to that given the real subjects — the quasi-controls are asked to respond or predict how they would have behaved if they were the actual subjects in the experiment. Because they do not experience the treatment variables, their data are based solely on their perceptions of the experimental situation. Similarity between the data from "nonexperiment" and "real" subjects indicates that the results *may* have been determined by the subjects' guesses about how they should respond rather than by any treatment effect. Thus the nonexperiment is an attempt to assess the extent to which the data are determined by the performance and role attitude cues transmitted to the subject by extraneous features of the experiment.

The use of the nonexperiment by Jackson and Pollard (1966) illustrates this technique. Introductory psychology students who had never participated in a sensory deprivation study were asked to predict the results of such an experiment described to them. They predicted that "real" subjects would overestimate the time spent in sensory deprivation, and a majority felt that performance would be poorer on posttreatment measures of cognitive, motor, and perceptual abilities. In addition, all but three of the subjects predicted one or more effects such as delusions, disorganized thoughts, or fears. Because the quasi-controls predicted much of the behavior typically associated with sensory deprivation, the possibility that the subjects' awareness and role attitudes *may* have determined these effects in previous studies cannot be ignored. Carefully designed procedures would be required to document the effects of sensory deprivation independent of these potential social contaminants.

The tentativeness of the interpretation based on the quasi-control data is noteworthy. The results *may* have been influenced by demand characteristics. It is impossible with the post-experiment inquiry, the nonexperiment, or with simulating subjects to conclusively demonstrate the existence of artifact. Such data merely indicate the likelihood that the results could have been determined by the subject's biased performance. However, the investigator may not conclude that his study demonstrated a particular phenomenon if the quasi-control data have indicated the subject's awareness and response to demand characteristics as a plausible explanation. Additional research is necessary to specify either the source of the artifact or the existence of the phenomenon.

SIMULATING SUBJECTS

The aware subject often deceives the experimenter about his awareness and cooperative attitude in order, presumably, to protect the validity of his participation. In the simulation quasi-control, this deceit is intentionally employed in an effort to assess the susceptibility of the research to subject bias. Subjects who do not receive or who are not likely to be affected by the experimental manipulations are asked to simulate the behavior of subjects who have. The extent to which simulators deceive the experimenter into thinking they are under the influence of these treatments suggests that the behavior of real subjects could also reasonably reflect what they perceive the experimenter desires.

Simulation has been used to demonstrate that hypnosis, though subject to social influences, is not entirely artifactually produced. A study by Orne, Sheehan, and Evans (1968) illustrates this application. They initially selected quasi-control subjects who would be uninfluenced by induction procedures — subjects scoring low on a scale of hypnotic susceptibility. These quasi-controls were asked to simulate behavior appropriate to the experiment. Along with the real subjects they experienced the standard induction. The critical response was a post-hypnotic suggestion to touch their forehead whenever the word "experiment" was mentioned by the hypnotist or by others outside the laboratory. The extent to which the experimenters were unable to discriminate simulators from actual subjects in the laboratory suggests that their hypnotic behavior may have been due to the subjects' awareness and desire to please the experimenter. However, the fact that only actual subjects who had been post-hypnotically induced demonstrated these behaviors outside the laboratory reveals that unique effects of hypnosis do exist. The reality of hypnotic phenomena has been suggested in other studies in which the behavior of simulators has been clearly different from that of hypnotized subjects. For example, the "accidental termination" of the experimental session and absence of the hypnotist appeared to remove the "hypnotic state" of simulators but not that of real subjects (Evans and Orne, 1971).

Simulation has had limited applicability as a quasi-control. For the most part it has been employed in the study of hypnosis to document the "realities" of trance states, post-hypnotic suggestions, and other hypnotic phenomena. Although its application to other research has not been explored, it should be useful where behavioral changes due to experimental treatments such as drugs, sensory restriction, and influence attempts are expected.

THE IMPACT OF QUASI-CONTROL DATA ON PSYCHOLOGICAL RESEARCH

The use of quasi-controls and their effect on research is best understood by an example of their application to the operant conditioning of verbal behavior. Years ago Thorndike (Thorndike and Rock, 1934) proposed that because reinforcements operate automatically, a person's behavior could be conditioned without his awareness. Following studies apparently documenting conditioning of verbal behavior without awareness (Greenspoon, 1955; Taffel, 1955), the potential of this form of control and modification for psychotherapy and other interpersonal situations became widely recognized. Most subsequent research has used the task employed in the Taffel study, in which subjects were required to make up a number of sentences employing a verb and one of six pronouns. The experimenter said "good" as reinforcement for each sentence that began with "I" or "we." An increase in the frequency of usage of these pronouns was taken as an index of conditioning. It was assumed that this occurred without awareness and was not merely compliance with the demands of the experiment. A number of psychologists questioned this assumption, suggesting that the subjects' conditioning performance was an artifact — the result of a common awareness and role attitude that produced only an apparent confirmation of the hypothesis. Because conclusive evidence for either view was not readily attainable, a controversy ensued. Most reinforcement theorists have argued that conditioning without awareness occurred (Greenspoon and Brownstein, 1967); many cognitive oriented psychologists favored the awareness interpretation (Spielberger and DeNike, 1966).

Obviously the answer had to be sought in the mental processes the subject used in his approach to the study. The post-experiment quasi-control has been extensively used for this purpose (Holmes, 1967; Spielberger, 1962). By requesting the subject to retrace the study, its performance cues, and his responses to them, it has been possible to assess the extent of conditioning or compliance with the demand characteristics of the situation. These studies have consistently revealed a relationship between awareness and conditioning performance; subjects who were aware were the only ones who "conditioned." A restructuring of the subjects' view of the experiment from the quasi-control data suggests what may be mediating the subject's behavior in this situation.

Contrary to the experimenter's intention, many *subjects* perceived the task as a "problem-solving game." Their job, it appeared, was to "solve the game" by discovering what made their sentences "good" (Holmes, 1967). Once they made this discovery, they indicated the solution to the problem by responding correctly. The absence of clear instructions and the gamelike presentation of the task apparently cued them to look for a solution. Because they wished to look good to the experimenter or to cooperate, they responded in a manner consistent with the experimenter's hypothesis. Although a few diehard reinforcement theorists argued that awareness occurred only because subjects had conditioned — that is, that the conditioned changes in behavior preceded awareness — the implications of the quasi-control data were clear: An alternative interpretation of the conditioning experiment was equally plausible. Conditioning without awareness could not be considered to have been conclusively demonstrated.

Thus data from the post-experiment questionnaires implied a need for more sophisticated research in which the influence of the demand characteristics of the experiment were reduced and this alternative explanation excluded. In other words, it was not denied that conditioning without awareness may occur — only that it had not been conclusively demonstrated in this context. The long-range effect of the quasi-control data has been to stimulate the improved designs found in recent research.

These studies have taken into account the potential role of demand characteristics. For example, to overcome the problem of awareness and problem-solving in one study subjects were required between conditioning trials to name as many different colors as they could. This reduced the opportunity for them to mentally explore what the experiment was about and apparently interfered with their problem-solving set and awareness of the correct hypothesis (Dixon and Oakes, 1965; Oakes, 1967), resulting in a demonstration of learning without awareness in a laboratory setting.

The same effect may be achieved in studies where subjects are unaware of their participation in an experiment. For example, in several conditioning studies with a unique twist, experimenters received reinforcements from confederates disguised as subjects. The exact form of the experimenter's reinforcement — whether he said "good," "yeah," or "uh-huh" — was conditioned by the "subjects" in one study (Rosenfeld and Baer, 1969). In another (Rosenfeld and Baer, 1970), the experimenter's task ostensibly was to condition the subjects' verbal behavior to decrease disfluencies in their pronunciation of a series of nouns — to get them to clearly say each noun, for example, "negotiation," without adding idiosyncratic speech sounds such as "uh, negotiation." In this case the confederates selectively reinforced the manner in which the experimenter requested the next noun. In both studies the "experimenters" were totally unaware that the frequency of their critical responses had been increased.

From studies of this sort it appears that conditioning without awareness occurs independent of subjects' knowledge of the hypothesis and compliance. "But" some will say, "this is the same conclusion we had before the fuss and bother with demand characteristics. Isn't this emphasis upon problems of awareness and compliance in the experiment merely a nuisance or deterrent to research progress — a methodological red herring?" Of course it is not. We have long ignored the "humanness" of our subject, recognized in the stress on demand characteristics and in the careful design of experiments that take into account awareness and compliance. Quasi-control data make us aware of this neglect and of the need for more careful research.

SUGGESTIONS FOR FURTHER READING

Quasi-Controls

Orne, M. T. 1969. Demand characteristics and the concept of quasi-controls. In *Artifact in behavioral research,* ed. R. Rosenthal and R. L. Rosnow, pp. 143–79. New York: Academic Press.

The concept of quasi-controls is developed, and the application of this technique to research problems is illustrated. In view of the similarities of demand characteristics in experiments to the placebo effect, quasi-controls are interpreted as analogous to the methods used in drug studies for dealing with this problem.

Post-Experiment Inquiry

Page, M. M. 1969. The social psychology of a classical conditioning of attitudes experiment. *Journal of personality and social psychology* 11: 177–86.

Page, M. M., and Scheidt, R. J. 1971. The elusive weapons effect: demand awareness, evaluation apprehension, and slightly sophisticated subjects. *Journal of personality and social psychology* 20: 304–09.

The use of the post-experiment questionnaire to assess the influence of subjects' awareness on research results is illustrated in these two studies. In the first, subjects' awareness and cooperation with the experimenter is posed as an alternative explanation of the classical conditioning of attitudes data. In the aggression study, post-experiment inquiry data suggest that subjects may have been reacting to the experiment's purposes rather than to the stimulating properties of the weapons.

Page, M. M. 1971. Post-experimental assessment of awareness in attitude conditioning. *Educational and psychological measurement* 31: 891–906.

The effect of the form of the inquiry on post-experiment questionnaire results is examined in this study. A greater correspondence between performance in the experiment and responses to the post-experiment inquiry is obtained with a more detailed questionnaire.

Simulation

Orne, M. T., and Evans, F. J. 1966. Inadvertent termination of hypnosis with hypnotized and simulating subjects. *International journal of clinical and experimental hypnosis* 14: 61–78.

The application of simulation as a quasi-control is illustrated by this study. It was found that simulators "awakened" when a power failure and the hypnotists' departure from the room terminated the hypnotic session and that real subjects remained in a trance.

Orne, M. T. 1971. The simulation of hypnosis: why, how, and what it means. *International journal of clinical and experimental hypnosis* 19: 183–210.

Simulation is a complex quasi-control technique; technical considerations in its application and what the data mean are explored in this paper.

The Nonexperiment

Stricker, G. 1967. A pre-experimental inquiry concerning cognitive determinants of emotional state. *Journal of general psychology* 76: 73–79.

An application of the nonexperiment to assess the extent to which two different experimental treatments for the arousal of emotional states are perceived differently by subjects.

Alexander, C. N., and Knight, G. W. 1971. Situated identities and social psychological experimentation. *Sociometry* 34: 65–82.

In this study a modified form of the nonexperiment quasi-control is applied to assess the extent to which subjects who hear a description of a study will respond like subjects within the study. Somewhat differently from Orne, however, the authors attribute this similarity to the commonly perceived socially desirable response for the situation. That is, both subjects and quasi-controls are looking for the form of their most desirable self-presentation.

CHAPTER SEVEN

Variations on the Experiment: Proposed Solutions to Subject Bias

Since the biasing effects of the subject's reactions to the laboratory have become widely recognized, modifications in experimental procedures have been proposed. Some of the proposals have been based on the assumption that if it can be assured that the subject will not discover the true purposes or dependent measures of an experiment, or even that he is in a study, his biased reactions to the laboratory will disappear. Thus, it has been proposed that studies be carefully disguised, that dependent measures not require the subjects' cooperation or conscious participation, and, in the extreme, that we abandon the laboratory and the peculiar reactions to it in favor of manipulations and observations in field experiments. At the other extreme it has been reasoned that one seldom rids an experiment of subjects' awareness. With an "If you can't lick 'em, join 'em" attitude, it has been proposed that the experimenter should capitalize on subjects' awareness and cooperation and solicit their active assistance in studying behavior. This radical departure from the approach of traditional research suggests that subjects should be told what the study is about and asked to indicate how they would have responded. There are pros and cons to each of these variations; their role in research and potential contributions should be carefully considered.

DECEPTION

Deception is often used to maintain or increase the subject's naiveté by presenting him with a number of performance cues that lead to incorrect hypotheses about the study. In other words, by lying about the purpose of the study, by providing misinformation about his own or another's behavior or personal attributes, or by employing deceptive apparatus, the investigator cues the subject to alternative hypotheses. When the resultant data are in accord with the experimenter's predictions, it is possible to conclude that the subjects' common hypotheses could not have accounted for the finding and that a true treatment effect exists. Unfortunately, deceptions are not always successful, and the ideal of uncontaminated data from naive subjects often is not achieved. Indeed, rather than aiding research, deception has often created methodological and ethical problems.

Methodological Problems

Effective deception requires considerable skill on the part of the experimenter and his confederates. Because many subjects view the experiment as a problem to be solved, they see quite easily through poorly acted deceptions, and as a result a certain percentage are aware not only of the purposes of the study but also that the experimenter has deceived them. With some subjects naive, others aware, and still others embittered by the deceit, assessing the results becomes difficult. In part results are dependent on the range of subjects' suspiciousness. In studies of conformity (Stricker, Messick, and Jackson, 1967; Adair, 1972a), significantly less yielding was found among suspicious subjects than among those who remained naive. In both of these studies, the degree of suspiciousness was quite high, ranging from 43 to 60 percent. With approximately half of the subjects suspicious of deception, conclusions about conformity behavior based on these studies are questionable.

Unfortunately, the direction of suspicious subjects' behavior varies with the study. They have been found to generally confirm the prediction in conditioning and persuasion studies and to disconfirm it in experiments on compliance and conformity (Weber and Cook, 1972). The direction of the behavior appears to be a function of the subjects' perceptions of the rationale for the hypothesis (Adair and Schachter, 1972) and the extent to which their defensive role attitudes have been aroused. If the subject believes the deception is designed to make a fool of him or that it challenges his abilities, a defensive reaction is a normal response. Under these conditions results are merely artifacts of the subjects' response to the performance and role attitude cues.

Part of the problem of deception stems from the difficulties of assessing awareness. On the one hand the investigator has a strong desire, if at times only latent, that his subjects will not be aware of the hypothesis. Combined with a lack of sophistication in the use of the post-experiment inquiry, assessment of awareness is often ineffective, if attempted at all. For example, Stricker (1967) surveyed deception in social psychological journals for one year and found an attempt to check the suspiciousness of subjects in only one-fourth of the studies. Although the maximum suspiciousness reported in any study was only 23 percent, it is doubtful that deceptions are generally that effective.

The foregoing problems are significant in light of the considerable research, particularly in social psychology, that employs deception and the recent suggestion that its use is increasing (Ring, 1967). Stricker (1967) found deception used in almost one-fifth of the studies in four major social psychological journals in 1964. Some phenomena by their very nature almost required the use of deception; 100 percent of the conformity studies involved deception about the performance of other subjects in the experiment. Similarly, experimenter expectancy effects are almost impossible to study without deceiving the "experimenters" about subjects they are testing.

Of greater concern than a particular deception experience is the generally negative or "deception-searching" attitude that results from the widespread use of the technique. Subjects who have experienced several deceptions respond to subsequent research with an entirely different orientation (Brock and Becker, 1966; Holmes and Appelbaum, 1970; Silverman, Schulman, and Wiesenthal, 1970). Although several studies designed to demonstrate the *gross* effects of deception have found that previously deceived subjects confirm the hypothesis less than naive subjects do, the precise effects of various degrees and types of prior deception under more subtle experimental conditions are not known. For example, Cook, Bean, Calder, Frey, Krovetz, and Reisman (1970) suggest that the effect of deception on the subject's subsequent approach to experiments is extremely complex and probably involves an interaction of variables such as the kinds and obviousness of deception, their justification, and the subjects' initial predisposition toward the experiment. Thus, not only has the investigator failed to resolve the problem of subjects' awareness and created for himself new methodological problems, but he has created for others and their subsequent research additional concerns.

These methodological problems have been considered by Stricker, Messick, and Jackson (1969). They concluded that although improvements may be made in inducing and assessing deceptions, suspicious subjects will always pose a problem. Because of the nature of the subject-experiment relationship, much of the experiment's purpose is not revealed and subjects become suspicious or wonder what the experimenter really intended. As a solution, Stricker, Messick, and Jackson propose detailed assessment of suspiciousness as a general practice and separate analysis of data according to the subjects' differential awareness of the experimenter's purposes.

Ethical Problems

To lie and deceive is a questionable practice that is even more questionable in the context of a personal contract between an experimenter and a subject. The subject is especially vulnerable. With the implicit support of the study by a university or research institute, there is pressure to believe whatever he is told. In thoughtlessly prepared experiments this may lead to unpleasant and occasionally harmful consequences to the subject. That these may be permanently damaging on rare occasions makes the use of deception of considerable concern (Kelman, 1967).

In particular Kelman points out that second-order deceptions — lies about the experimental context — are a special problem and their use should be almost universally abhorred. A study within a university setting illustrates this problem. The study was designed to explore the lasting effects of experimental deceptions on students (Lowin and Ingraham, 1968). However, subjects were deceived not only about their own behavior but about the existence of a university counseling service as well. At the beginning of the year, a group of male freshman students were counseled for thirty minutes and "with conviction" that their performance on the university's entrance examinations clearly suggested they were capable of barely passable academic performance. In the concluding remarks of the session, the subjects were asked to consider alternatives to their present academic plans "including changing curricula, school, even the army." Immediately after personal reactions were obtained, subjects were debriefed and told that the counseling service was nonexistent and that the advice they had received was manufactured. The potential harm to the subjects was in no way offset by the noble purposes of the study. It is difficult to imagine a subject, initially uncertain about college, who would reveal through that same "counselor" or for that matter any bona fide counseling center, the lasting psychological scars he received as a result of this deception. Surprisingly, the authors expressed concern that an occasional student who is permanently affected by the deception may remain undetected by their group statistical techniques; yet they failed to indicate their recognition that their experiment could conceivably include such subjects.

Deception to remove the problems of subjects' awareness is a dubious technique, to be used only with extreme caution when essential and to be abandoned if found to be ineffectual (Ring, 1967; McGuire, 1967). Advances in experimental methodology are required to prevent psychologists from being placed in such methodologically unsound and ethically unjustified positions as deception implies.

ROLE-PLAYING AS AN ALTERNATIVE
TO DECEPTION

In response to these methodological and ethical concerns, Kelman (1967) has suggested a search for alternative methods that utilize the subject's motivations to understand and to contribute to research. If, as has been implied, we will never rid the experiment of the problem of the subject's awareness, then why not employ the reverse strategy — actively involve the subject as a fully aware partner in a joint research effort? Instead of deceiving the subject, we would level with him and seek his assistance in "conscientiously taking the roles and carrying out the tasks the experimenter assigns to him." Of several approaches Kelman considered, role-playing appeared to be the most promising alternative.

In this technique the entire experiment is revealed to the subject, and he is asked to play a role and provide data for the experimenter. In some studies subjects are asked to play the role of participants in psychological experiments (Greenberg, 1967); in others, they may take the role of key officials in various countries (Guetzkow, Alger, Brody, Noel, and Snyder, 1963) or of buyers and sellers of used cars (Chertkoff and Conley, 1967). Role-playing has been used in many studies of bargaining and of cooperation versus competition as an alternative to the traditional deception experiment (Rapoport and Chammah, 1965; Deutsch and Krauss, 1960). In other studies it has been used with traditional techniques (Horowitz and Rothschild, 1970; Willis and Willis, 1970) in which the behavior of the experimental subjects is compared with that of role-playing subjects. The intention, of course, is that comparability of these sets of data will eventually permit the use of role-playing as a substitute for the deception experiment.

Fundamental to role-playing in each of these contexts is the assumption that the subject playing a particular role will yield data comparable to behavior in the real world or, at a minimum, comparable to behavior in the typical psychological experiment. This may occur whenever the subject becomes so involved in his participation that he forgets that he is merely playing a role. When the task is engrossing and lends itself to intense subject involvement, the role is easily adopted, and the behavior called for appears meaningful to the subject. On the other hand, when asked to role-play subjects or to respond to somewhat inconsequential manipulations (Greenberg, 1967; Willis and Willis, 1970), subjects become aware of their task, are forced to think through the situation to figure out how they or other subjects would respond, and yield data that are guesses at behavior rather than real behavior. Under these conditions "psychology by consensus" (Freedman, 1969) is of dubious value.

This problem may be illustrated by a role-played "replication" of Schachter's study (1959) of anxiety and affiliation (Greenberg, 1967). Subjects were given the same anxiety-provoking or calming instructions and shock apparatus used by Schachter to observe its effects on their affiliative response. Following the instructions, the role-playing subjects were successively asked to indicate the degree of anxiety they would have felt to the instructions and shock equipment and what preference they would have for waiting alone or with someone else until the next part of the experiment. Schachter had found that subjects who received anxiety-producing instructions preferred to wait together, particularly if they were first-born. Greenberg obtained essentially similar results and concluded that his study confirmed the validity of the role-playing technique as an alternative to deception.

There are difficulties with this interpretation. First, it seems likely that role-playing subjects would have had difficulty "getting into the role." Not only did they know they would never receive the shock, but going into an experiment to role-play subjects in another experiment has an air of artificiality twice removed. In addition to the inappropriateness of asking subjects to role-play subjects, the similarity of this approach to the non-experiment quasi-control should be noted. Asking subjects to respond *as if* they were subjects in an experiment elicits their view of the demand characteristics. Thus, a quasi-control interpretation of the similarity between Schachter's and Greenberg's data would be that the former observation could have been determined by the demand characteristics of the experiment. Role-playing of this sort could certainly not also be considered as an alternative research method.

This has not been intended as an indictment of role-playing. Certainly gaming research has profitably studied bargaining, cooperation, competition, and other interpersonal processes. Under the conditions described earlier, certain data from role-playing experiments may be useful. What is needed are studies to ascertain the ecological validity of the technique. Comparisons with other experimental tasks (Sermat, 1970; Horowitz and Rothschild, 1970; Willis and Willis, 1970) may show the comparability of role-playing to behavior in traditional experiments, but the generalizability of laboratory data to real life must be ascertained. Evidence of this sort is difficult to obtain, and it will take some time before it may be determined that modifying the traditional subject-experimenter relationship to include role-playing is an *independent,* legitimate alternative. At present, it appears more likely that role-playing, like the nonexperiment quasi-controls, will be useful in clarifying our understanding of experiments but will "not supplant the need for substantive research" (Orne, 1970).

NATURALISTIC RESEARCH AS AN ALTERNATIVE TO THE LABORATORY

We have focused on the effect of demand characteristics within the experimental laboratory. For the most part, these effects are due to the subject's recognition that he is in an experiment, and this realization somehow changes his behavior. If it were possible to study behavior in a naturalistic setting without this awareness, the problems associated with demand characteristics would presumably disappear. Unaware he is in a study, the subject's problem-solving set and strong motivation to comply or to look good would not be aroused. He would not find himself in a strange environment and would not feel the need for performance and role attitude cues to guide his behavior. His behavior would not be contaminated by his attitudes toward psychologists and research. This possibility has led many psychologists to naturalistic research.

An example of meaningful research that can take place outside of the laboratory is Wrightsman's study (1969) of issues arising in the United States presidential election of 1968. Law and order was made a salient issue in that campaign by George Wallace. Whether his supporters were more or less law-abiding than those of other candidates became an interesting behavioral question. To test this, Wrightsman examined in Tennessee whether persons who identified themselves by bumper stickers as supporters of one of the candidates had also displayed the required Davidson County, Tennessee, automobile tax stamp. He found significantly less frequent law-abiding behavior (display of the tax stamp) among Wallace supporters than among those who favored Nixon, Humphrey, or no candidate. The tax stamps and bumper stickers provided nonreactive, valid measures of behavior and preferences. Indeed, not only was the subject not required to respond to the investigator; he was not even present when the data were collected. Although this example is somewhat ingenious, a considerable amount of meaningful research can be conducted through the use of such nonreactive measures and field techniques that are readily available.

But one should not get the feeling that the advantages of naturalistic research áre not countered by disadvantages. For example, the manipulatory control to which we have become accustomed in the laboratory is no longer available. Often variables that would ordinarily have been controlled in a laboratory investigation are co-acting if not interacting with the variable under investigation in the "real" environment. Investigators of naturalistic phenomena frequently find that they must wait for natural events to occur before certain behaviors may be studied. For example, Wrightsman could not have conducted his study without certain issues' being salient during an election year. Similarly it is feasible to study the reactions to national catastrophes, such as the assassination of John F. Kennedy, only when those events occur.

To handle some of these problems, investigators have manipulated the environment to create desired behavioral events. This was done in a study of the extent to which individuals in different countries falsely claimed another's money as their own (Feldman, 1968). Systematically selected subjects on the streets of three major cities were individually approached from behind by the investigator, who queried, "Excuse me, sir. Did you just drop this dollar bill?" The subject's response, socio-economic status (crudely determined by a dress-classification scheme), and even post-experiment inquiry data were recorded without the subject's knowledge that he had participated in an experiment. The post-experiment inquiry was conducted by another investigator who "happened" to be walking beside the subject as the experimental episode ended. He began his interview with the remark, "Hey, is that guy giving money away?" and then proceeded to explore the subject's view of the incident. Problems of subject bias and most inadequacies of naturalistic research were circumvented. The ethics of conducting this kind of naturalistic deception experiment, however, leave the investigator with other dilemmas.

Naturalistic investigations are not entirely free of social contaminants. In the method of participant observation, in which the investigator attempts to unobtrusively observe while participating within a group, the observer occasionally may inadvertently influence the behavior of his subjects. In one study of this sort the observer, as a member of a "doomsday" group, was called upon to mediate between God and the group as the hour of doom approached (Festinger, Riecken, and Schachter, 1956). He was chosen because he had come to have the faith from outside the group. Unfortunately for his scientific observations, almost anything he would say would influence the behavior of the group he was observing.

In some naturalistic experiments subjects interact with the experimenter or his confederates in unplanned ways. For example, Bryan and Test (1967) encountered unusual difficulty with subjects' interacting with a "lady in distress." In their study, a young lady and her car with a flat tire were strategically located on a Los Angeles street. The number of drivers who stopped and offered assistance, under model conditions (a confederate assisting another lady in distress a distance ahead of the test car) and no-model conditions, was recorded. In more than a few instances, however, the subjects attempted to "pick up" the young lady and were not readily discouraged even by the knowledge that she was part of a psychological experiment. The apparent altruistic or helping behavior in reality was amorously motivated. This looseness in naturalistic research is offset to some extent by the total absence of the subjects' awareness of their participation in an experiment. Without alternatives the investigators must weigh the relative merits and pitfalls of research in the laboratory and in the field.

Naturalistic research methods achieve what the psychologist has been unable to accomplish in the laboratory — systematic study of human behavior without the problem of subject awareness and other forms of subject and experimenter bias. However, disadvantages to naturalistic research must be carefully considered. At present the only guide to the selection of a method is the needs and problems of the investigation in question. Perhaps by attacking the problem from converging methodologies — that is, through the laboratory experiment, role-playing, and field study — we may learn something about our methods as well as about behavior.

SUGGESTIONS FOR FURTHER READING

Deception

Stricker, L. J.; Messick, S.; and Jackson, D. N. 1969. Evaluating deception in psychological research. *Psychological bulletin* 71: 343–51.

Reviewing studies on the use of deception and evaluating its effectiveness, the authors recommend ways in which the methodological problems associated with deception may be minimized.

Kelman, H. C. 1967. Human use of human subjects: the problem of deception in social psychological experiments. *Psychological bulletin* 67: 1–11.

This classic article signaled the dangers and implication of continued and widespread use of deception.

Orne, M. T., and Holland, C. 1968. On the ecological validity of laboratory deceptions. *International journal of psychiatry* 6: 282–93.

Through a careful analysis of Milgram's studies in obedience the authors illustrate the importance of evaluating how the subject perceives the experiment and its deceptions before meaningful inferences may be drawn from the laboratory to life outside the experiment.

Role-playing

Miller, A. G. 1972. Role playing: an alternative to deception? A review of the evidence. *American psychologist* 27: 623–36.

Limited to a consideration of role-playing only as an alternative to deception and to a review of four empirical studies, the author concluded that the prospects for this technique are poor.

Freedman, J. L. 1969. Role playing: psychology by consensus. *Journal of personality and social psychology* 13: 107–14.

The author takes the view that the subjects' consensus of how they would have behaved in a role-played study is not a valid substitute for observations of their behavior.

Field Research

Bickman, L., and Henchy, T., eds. 1972. *Beyond the laboratory: field research in social psychology.* New York: McGraw-Hill.

An examination of this collection of forty-five studies reveals the variety of behavior that may be studied in the field if the investigator applies his ingenuity to devising the appropriate methods.

Evans, R. I., and Rozelle, R. M., eds. 1970. *Social psychology in life.* Boston: Allyn & Bacon.

Included in this anthology is research in which the investigator has manipulated real-life settings, recorded behavior through participant observation, and independently analyzed an event that had recently occurred. The articles illustrate the range of approaches outside of the laboratory.

Snadowsky, A. M., ed. 1972. *Social psychology research: laboratory-field relationships.* New York: Free Press.

This anthology for students of social psychology illustrates the need for a balance of methods in our attack on research problems. Field and laboratory research on the same topic are presented so that their respective contributions to the development of knowledge may be noted.

Willems, E. P., and Rausch, H. L., eds. 1969. *Naturalistic viewpoints in psychological research.* New York: Holt, Rinehart and Winston.

For some research problems the study of behavior in its natural setting is the most appropriate strategy. This view of naturalistic research is presented in this collection of articles.

Nonreactive Research

Seechest, L. 1969. Nonreactive assessment of attitudes. In *Naturalistic viewpoints in psychological research,* ed. E. P. Willems and H. L. Raush, pp. 147–61. New York: Holt, Rinehart and Winston.

By using methods that avoid the subject's awareness, that do not require his cooperation, and that do not alter the phenomenon being studied, it is possible to meaningfully infer attitudes. Such unobtrusive measures do not suffer from the subjects' reactivity to self-report measures.

Webb, E. J.; Campbell, D. T.; Schwartz, R. D.; and Seechrest, L. 1966. *Unobtrusive measures: nonreactive research in the social sciences.* New York: Rand McNally.

The advantages and limitations of the use of archives, observations, and physical traces of prior behavior as nonreactive measures in the social sciences are explored. Generous examples of each technique are provided.

CHAPTER EIGHT

Ethical Considerations

The psychologist's exploration and manipulation of behavior create another concern — the ethics of research with human subjects. At the root of this concern is the conflict of the individual's rights and needs with those of others. In the experiment, the "right" to study, to manipulate, or to examine is conferred upon psychologists by society in accord with its needs for greater understanding of man and his behavior. The "right" of the individual to have a choice in his experiences, to reveal to others only what he wishes to reveal, to feel secure that his personal shortcomings may be known only to himself, have long been assured. The investigation of behavior, however, inherently violates these rights and, with developments and technological advances in psychological research, has increasingly come into conflict with the right of the individual to maintain his privacy.

The resolution of this conflict is not to be found in the absolute authority of individual rights or in the complete freedom of the psychologist to investigate behavior as he pleases. A compromise is required, and the desired balance is between the significance of the particular investigation for society weighed against minimal discomfort and violation of individual rights. To achieve a balance of benefit and risk the psychologist must be sensitive to potential ethical issues and respond to them in accordance with the principles established for the profession (American Psychological Association, 1963).[1] But this balance is not readily at-

[1] The code of ethics for the American Psychological Association has had several trial versions and has been revised in response to advances in techniques and knowledge. The

tained. The APA code of ethics does not provide specific rules of conduct for every situation. The uniqueness of each interpersonal encounter precludes a routine response and requires that each experiment be examined from the perspective of the rights of both the individual and the investigator.

Certain considerations must be included in this ethical review. Wolfensberger (1967) proposed that four critical considerations are essential — obtaining the subject's consent, the subject's rights yielded to the investigator, types of research, and risks to the subject. His analysis leads to guidelines that provide for specified ethical responses when certain conditions of experimentation, risk, and yielded rights are present. Informed consent is the cornerstone of research ethics, yet what subjects are told is necessarily contingent upon what they are able to understand. The subject may have personal limitations — he may be retarded or emotionally disturbed — or the type of study may be so complex that to fully communicate its purposes is impossible. Indeed, under certain circumstances, the investigator may choose not to disclose what the study is about if such knowledge would vitiate his results. His decision not to obtain fully informed consent, however, should be based on the assumption that the rights and risks asked of the subject are not excessive. In other words, the appropriate ethical response is contingent upon the unique conditions of the investigation under consideration.

Even ethical decisions following these guidelines will not be easy. What one person may consider an ethically "clean" study may not appear so to another investigator or to subjects. A study that strikingly illustrates this point has been described by Clark (1967). An investigator was conducting a door-to-door survey in a typical residential neighborhood. His procedure was to ask each housewife a number of questions related to her use of contraceptive devices. The questions led to detailed answers that one might have thought would be beyond the limits of what an individual would choose to reveal. Surprisingly, however, all respondents cooperated — at least until the interviewer's final question. At that point the subjects felt their privacy was being invaded, and they indignantly refused to answer. The question was, "How much money does your husband make a year?" Much to the investigator's surprise, the topic he felt to be dangerously close to invasion of privacy had yielded highly co-

---

present code has been elaborated and interpreted (American Psychological Association, 1967a) and is currently undergoing careful reexamination (American Psychological Association, 1968) in preparation for further revisions. The latest proposed revisions (Cook, Kimble, Hicks, McGuire, Schoggen, and Smith, 1971) suggest that the code may introduce even greater protection of individual rights.

operative responses, and the question that appeared to be less offensive was seen as an invasion of privacy. The explanation for the respondents' behavior was rational. They had, before the interview began, consented to answer questions related to their use of contraceptive devices. On the final question, however, the interviewer had stepped out of line; he had asked something they had not consented to answer. He had invaded their privacy without permission. Thus what appears to the investigator to be proper and ethical may not appear that way to the subject.

This suggests that ethical considerations in any potentially sensitive study should be reviewed by an independent, unbiased qualified observer. With this in mind the United States Public Health Service, in a policy statement of the Surgeon General (American Psychological Association, 1967*b*), stipulated that a *prior* ethical review would be mandatory for all PHS-sponsored research and that it would be conducted by a committee of the investigator's institutional colleagues. Implicit in this policy is the assumption that although the individual scientist may be in a poor position to judge the ethical shortcomings of his research, his peers will generally have a more objective view. All too often individual psychologists fail to recognize the personal human element in their research, to the detriment of their relationship to subjects. Clearly, we will ultimately pay for this failure. We must become *overly* concerned with the personal nature of our research, to ensure that we bring into balance the rights of science and the rights of the individual.

SUGGESTIONS FOR FURTHER READING

General Reviews

Graubard, S. R., ed. 1969. Ethical aspects of experimentation with human subjects. *Daedalus* 98, no. 2.

The philosophical, sociological, legal, and governmental aspects of the ethics of research with human subjects are considered in this collection of papers. Although the emphasis is on medical research, problems associated with psychological, sociological, and anthropological study are considered.

Sasson, R., and Nelson, T. M. 1969. The human experimental subject in context. *Canadian psychologist* 10: 409–37.

In this thorough review of the ethical issues arising from manipulations that affect the safety, comfort, privacy, and personal dignity of human subjects, special consideration is given to the role of human experimentation in the university context.

Guidelines for Research with Human Subjects

Cook, S.; Kimble, G. A.; McGuire, W. J.; Hicks, L. H.; Schoggen, P. H. and Smith, M. B. 1972. Ethical standards for research with human subjects. *APA monitor* 3: i–xx.

In this article are the ten ethical principles proposed as guidelines for the American Psychological Association. Although the proposed code is quite brief, the considerations that were given to each point prior to its formulation provide insights into the researcher-subject ethical dilemma.

Wolfensberger, W. 1967. Ethical issues in research with human subjects. *Science* 155: 47–51.

This is a careful analysis, from the researcher's point of view, of the elements involved in an ethical evaluation of human research. Emphasis is on the potential impact of ethical decisions on the conduct of research.

Baumrind, D. 1971. Principles of ethical conduct in the treatment of subjects: reaction to the draft report of the Committee on Ethical Standards in Psychological Research. *American psychologist* 26: 887–96.

Looking at the ethical dilemma from the individual's perspective, Baumrind rejects the proposed APA code for not providing adequate protection of fundamental human rights. In contrast to the view that an individual's rights may be violated if the significance of the research warrants it, she argues that the investigator should compromise in his choice of methods.

Guidelines for Drug Research

American Psychological Association. 1972. Guidelines for psychologists for the use of drugs in research. *American psychologist* 27: 335–36.

With the contemporary use and interest in drugs, principles were required to guide the conduct of research into their effects.

Guidelines for Sensitivity Training

Lakin, M. 1969. Ethical issues in sensitivity training. *American psychologist* 24: 923–28.

The author examines the elements of sensitivity training that affect the individual and public welfare and that place the trainer into numerous ethical dilemmas. The need for professional standards is emphasized.

Guidelines for Psychological Testing

Amrine, M., ed. 1965. Testing and public policy. *American psychologist* (Special Issue) 20: 859–988.

The focus of the special issue is the 1965 congressional inquiry into testing. This inquiry and related articles disclose the numerous ethical dilemmas encountered in personality, aptitude, and intelligence testing.

American Psychological Association. 1970. Psychological assessment and public policy. *American psychologist* 25: 264–66.

In response to attacks on the extensive use of psychological tests in schools, business, and research, and on psychological assessment generally as an invasion of privacy, the American Psychological Association prepared this position statement. Emphasizing the need for properly qualified examiners to select and administer the appropriate test, the statement also proposes general guidelines to govern the examiner-examinee relationship.

CHAPTER NINE

Implications for Future Research

What can we conclude about future research with human subjects? Most attempts to resolve the fundamental problems have followed
one of two courses. On the one hand there have been pressures to change
our relationships with subjects by involving them as research collaborators. Although only a modification in our approach, its implications for
the laboratory experiment must be carefully considered. In contrast there
have been efforts to buttress the natural science model of experimentation by ensuring the naive objectivity of the research subject.

Attempts to preserve the passive, naive subject have included better
concealed, more elaborate deceptions, unobtrusive or nonreactive dependent measures, and abandoning the laboratory in order to conduct
research in a naturalistic setting where the subject is unaware that he
is in an experiment. These approaches have limitations — in the kinds of
behavior that can be studied with unobtrusive or nonreactive measures
or in the field, and in a lack of tolerance for deception. Clearly the ethical and methodological reservations against the use of deception and the
limits of what can be studied by field research contribute to a Zeitgeist
that inclines more toward changes than toward preservation of the traditional relationship between experimenter and subject.

RELATIONSHIP WITH SUBJECTS

At the outset it was clear that this methodological research was motivated by an underlying dissatisfaction with the overly mechanistic laboratory approach to the study of human behavior. The rigorous application

of the experimental method failed to yield all the data required for an understanding of behavior. In particular, exclusion of the subject as an active research participant limited our knowledge of his perceptions and intentions. To many psychologists the frustration of studying human subjects without "talking" to them was the mirror image of Watson's frustration in having to introspect for his rats. Indeed these contemporary concerns and proposed solutions appear to reintroduce to the research process the very human qualities Watson had extracted from the experiment.

The research we have considered has recognized the potency of the subjects' awareness of his participation in an experiment and has attempted to reintroduce verbal report of his thoughts and feelings as a necessary and legitimate component of the experiment. The thrust of the proposed methodological changes has been toward involving the subject in the research process — that is, altering his role to that of a more active participant.

Pressures for Change

This new role began quite innocuously with the suggestion of increased post-experiment participation by the subject to aid in understanding laboratory behavior. Alternative quasi-control techniques such as simulation and the nonexperiment further involved subjects to obtain their view of the experiment. Nevertheless, their involvement was limited to what we might call supra-experimental data — data gathered *after* their participation as subjects was completed or as an *additional* "control" group. Thus, although quasi-control data came from "involved" subjects, it has always been considered an aid to understanding the experiment, not primary data.

Radical proposed changes would alter the data collection process itself. For example, some have suggested that we involve the subject as a research assistant who makes a significant and active contribution to the study (Argyris, 1968; Weber and Cook, 1972). Subjects would be trained to adopt the "proper" orientation toward the experiment in order to produce "bias-free" data or at least signal when data are biased. That specific attitudes toward the experiment may be trained into subjects has been empirically demonstrated (Earn, 1971); however, what constitutes the "proper" attitude is not clear. Equally extreme in its involvement of the subject in the collection of data is the technique of role-playing (Kelman, 1967). Although proposed as a substitute for deception, it has been considered by many to be a viable alternative to any traditional laboratory experiment.

Consistent with these methodological pressures is our sharpened awareness of ethical considerations in research with human subjects. The proposed changes in the American Psychological Association's Code of Ethics (Cook, Kimble, Hicks, McGuire, Schoggen, and Smith, 1971) would require informed consent prior to participation. Subjects would have to be aware of many of the procedures and purposes of the study that investigators in the past have worked hard to avoid disclosing. Although this could be waived if the subject's awareness would influence his results, the implications of the proposed "ideal" relationship are clear: Many traditional procedures are ethically unsound and may be used only with this recognition; alternatives that permit the subject greater understanding of his role in the experiment should be sought and utilized. Although the version that will be adopted by the APA may be changed on this point, some take a more militant view of our ethical relations with subjects (Baumrind, 1971). Baumrind feels that what we disclose to the subject to obtain his consent would still not reveal all that we should. She favors a complete disclosure in which we treat our subjects as collaborators rather than as objects and thus achieve a "creative transformation of the structure of scientific research."

The Involved Subject

The cumulative effect of these pressures from both methodological and ethical sources would be a greater involvement of the subject in research. In contrast to his current role as a passive object for study, it appears likely that the "new" subject would be asked to consent to participate in a study in which he has full knowledge and for which he has been trained to report his biases and behavioral experiences. He would no longer be an outsider who is manipulated and coerced but would be asked to assist the experimenter in a partnership in which he not only provided behavioral data but indicated as best he could the presence of extraneous influences. His thoughts, feelings, and perceptions of the experiment would become of concern and his views sought to improve and refine the study. It is difficult to conceive of a total alteration of the philosophy underlying human research, as the phenomenologists desire, but a trend toward greater involvement of the subject within the experimental tradition appears a real possibility.

A Changing Zeitgeist

Acceptance of this requires a change in the Zeitgeist — a greater tolerance and acceptance of a new role for subjects. The development of a

Zeitgeist for change was discussed in Chapter 1. Dissatisfaction with the applicability of the traditional research approach, the emergence of a questioning, anti-establishment attitude, and concern for the relevance of research to the solution of man's problems in the world have combined to produce a tolerance, even a hope, for new methods. Added to this is an increasing concern for the preservation of the individual. We live in a mass society in which people are numbers and individual rights are often yielded for the common good. Thus research in which an individual's perceptions and thoughts are given prime consideration is readily accepted by many psychologists.

As a consequence there is already some evidence of a changing relationship with subjects. A tally of the articles in the recent volumes of the prominent social psychology journals reveals increasing references to the problems raised by this methodological research. Many studies have been designed to exclude experimenter or subject bias, and a number have employed one of the quasi-control techniques as a method of solution. It is also noteworthy that these references extend beyond the research in which the techniques originated — for example, hypnosis and sensory deprivation — into experimental areas such as perception, learning, and physiological psychology.

A similar trend has been observed in the acceptance and application of role-playing and the nonexperiment to a greater number and variety of research problems. In research on self-persuasion, dissonance, and attitude change, their use has been extensive (Bem, 1967). There have also been modifications in our treatment of subjects in compulsory subject pools. Special efforts to more adequately debrief subjects and to fulfill our ethical responsibility by ensuring that they are aware of their option to withdraw from a study if it becomes offensive to them (King, 1970; Menges, 1971) have been instituted in some universities as guidelines for the use of compulsory subjects. There also appears to be a trend toward increased participation by subjects in ethical review procedures, although no published data support this observation.

ANOTHER TURN IN THE
SPIRAL OF HISTORY?

Greater consideration of subjects' thoughts, feelings, and verbalizations, of their interpretation of the experimental situation, and their central role in research are reminiscent of the role and activities of subjects who participated as observers in introspective psychology. The resemblance extends beyond efforts to explore subjects' thought processes, to training subjects to adopt the proper attitude and to depend on their verbal report as primary data. This similarity should not be surprising.

Scientific developments tend to follow a recurrent pattern — not a repetition of older ideas but a spiraling effect in which improvements are added and a greater sophistication is built on older conceptualizations. Thus the contemporary proposals may be a progression to a more sophisticated methodology — the next turn in the spiral of history. By placing in juxtaposition the contemporary proposals with both the earlier introspection and the mode of experimenter-subject relationship that has prevailed for the past fifty years, we may discern potential advances that lie before us and pitfalls we should avoid.

On the positive side it appears that the questions asked of the contemporary subject are more behavioral and have more relevance to real life than those Wundt and Titchener asked their observers. Certainly these proposals advocate a more balanced mixture of behavioral and verbal reports and a more supplementary role for the subject's introspections than was true of the earlier psychology. Compared with the prominent role of the experimenter in behavioristic and of the subject in introspective psychology, the new experimenter-subject relationship achieves a fine balance. Indeed this moderation of earlier excesses suggests that the concerns we have been considering may be leading to a maturing rather than to a drastic change of our methods.

On the other hand certain aspects of the new proposals so resemble negative features of the earlier psychology that caution against their uncritical acceptance is advised. This is especially true of techniques in which the "new" subject plays a more prominent role in personally yielding primary behavioral data — for example, by role-playing — and in training subjects to adopt the "proper" attitude toward experiments. The difficulty of assessing what constitutes a "proper" attitude and the greater dependence on the subject than on the research design for primary behavioral data are problems that plagued the early introspectionists. Extensive research on the validity of these new techniques is needed.

One other change in our methodological approach seems warranted by the diversity of the problems we have examined. It is rather clear that our methods are imperfect and, though we may improve them, they probably will remain so. We are just as likely to encounter bias in the field as in the laboratory, in the role-played study as in the carefully prepared deception, in samples available in the university or solicited from the general public, in verbal reports, and in behavioral measures. Only by employing "converging methodologies" may we ensure a valid understanding of behavior. Although this occurs to some extent incidentally through variations in approach of researchers from different laboratories, systematic convergence on a research problem with different methods and measures in different settings would appear to be a wise scientific strategy.[1] Researchers have long argued for the importance of replication as a verification of their observations. "Convergent replication," in which the same problem is examined by different methods, would be a more potent strategem.

CONCLUDING REMARKS

The methodological concerns expressed in this research on the social psychology of the psychological experiment have been viewed by many as critical and even destructive of the experimental method. They were not intended to be so. For the most part, the foregoing research has been supportive of the model yet critical of its application. Precision in the psychological laboratory requires consideration of its *human* subject matter and the social context in which research occurs. Consideration of the subjects' and experimenters' motives and perceptions in the design of research and in the selection of samples and the addition of quasi-control and expectancy control groups to assess experimenter and subject bias are merely necessary precautions. Precise human research is difficult. It would be less difficult and more precise if we remembered that it was *human*.

SUGGESTIONS FOR FURTHER READING

Webb, E. J.; Campbell, D. T.; Schwartz, R. D.; and Seechrest, L. 1966. *Unobtrusive measures: nonreactive research in the social sciences.* New York: Rand McNally, pp. 1–34.

In their opening chapter the authors suggest multiple operationism as a research strategy. Their emphasis, of course, is on unobtrusive measures as a supplement to interviews and questionnaires.

[1] A similar suggestion has been made by Webb, Campbell, Schwartz, and Seechrest (1966), who have argued for "multiple operationism, a collection of methods combined to avoid sharing the same weaknesses" (pp. 1–2). It is their hope that unobtrusive or nonreactive measures may supplement and cross-validate — that is, serve as a check upon — the conclusions obtained by interviews and questionnaires.

References

Adair, J. G. 1970*a*. Pre-experiment attitudes toward psychology as a determinant of experimental results: verbal conditioning of aware subjects. *Proceedings of the 78th annual convention of the American Psychological Association* 5: 417–18.

——. 1970*b*. Pre-experiment attitudes toward psychology as a determinant of subject behavior. Paper presented in the symposium entitled "Methodological problems in research with human subjects" at the annual meeting of the Canadian Psychological Association, May 1970, Winnipeg, Canada.

——. 1972*a*. Demand characteristics or conformity? Suspiciousness of deception and experimenter bias in conformity research. *Canadian journal of behavioural science* 4: 238–48.

——. 1972*b*. Volunteer vs. coerced subjects. *American psychologist* 27: 508.

Adair, J. G., and Epstein, J. 1968. Verbal cues in the mediation of experimenter bias. *Psychological reports* 22: 1045–53.

Adair, J. G., and Fenton, D. P. 1971. Subject's attitudes toward psychology as a determinant of experimental results. *Canadian journal of behavioural science* 3: 268–75.

Adair, J. G., and Schachter, B. S. 1972. To cooperate or to look good? Subjects' and experimenters' perceptions of each other's intentions. *Journal of experimental social psychology* 8: 74–85.

American Psychological Association. 1963. Ethical standards of psychologists. *American psychologist* 18: 56–60.

——. 1967*a*. *Casebook on ethical standards of psychologists*. Washington, D.C.

——. 1967*b*. Surgeon General's directives on human experimentation. *American psychologist* 22: 350–55.

——. 1968. Ethical issues in psychological research. Forthcoming survey of APA members: a letter to the membership. *American psychologist* 23: 689–90.

Anderson, O. D. 1930. An experimental study of observational attitudes. *American journal of psychology* 42: 345–69.

Angell, J. R. 1913. Behavior as a category of psychology. *Psychological review* 20: 255–70.

Argyris, C. 1968. Some unintended consequences of rigorous research. *Psychological bulletin* 70: 185–97.

Aronson, E., and Cope, V. 1968. My enemy's enemy is my friend. *Journal of personality and social psychology* 8: 8–12.

Baldwin, J. M. 1895. Studies from the Princeton laboratory. IV. Types of reactions. *Psychological review* 2: 259–73.

Barber, T. X., and Silver, M. J. 1968. Fact, fiction, and the experimenter bias effect. *Psychological bulletin monograph supplement* 70: 1–29.

Barr, A. S. 1932. A study of the amount of agreement found in the results of four experimenters employing the same experimental techniques in a study of the effects of visual and auditory stimulation on learning. *Journal of educational research* 26: 35–45.

Baumrind, D. 1971. Principles of ethical conduct in treatment of subjects: reaction of the draft report of the Committee on Ethical Standards in Psychological Research. *American psychologist* 26: 887–96.

Bem, D. J. 1967. Self-perception: an alternative interpretation of cognitive dissonance phenomena. *Psychological review* 74: 183–200.

Bentley, M. 1929. "Observer" and "subject." *American journal of psychology* 41: 682–83.

Black, R. W.; Schumpert, J.; and Welch, F. 1972. Partial reinforcement extinction effect in perceptual-motor performance: coerced versus volunteer subject populations. *Journal of experimental psychology* 92: 143–45.

Bode, B. H. 1922. What is psychology? *Psychological review* 29: 250–58.

Bogdonoff, M. D.; Brehm, L.; and Back, K. 1964. The effect of the experimenter's role upon the subject's response to an unpleasant task. *Journal of psychosomatic research* 8: 137–43.

Boring, E. G. 1950. *A history of experimental psychology.* 2nd ed. New York: Appleton-Century-Crofts.

——. 1953. A history of introspection. *Psychological bulletin* 50: 169–89.

Bouchard, T. J., Jr., and Hare, H. 1970. Size, performance and potential in brainstorming groups. *Journal of applied psychology* 54: 51–55.

Bridgman, P. W. 1927. *The logic of modern physics.* New York: Macmillan.

Brock, T. C., and Becker, L. A. 1966. "Debriefing" and susceptibility to subsequent experimental manipulations. *Journal of experimental social psychology* 2: 314–23.

Brower, C. 1948. The role of incentive in psychological research. *Journal of general psychology* 39: 145–47.

Brunswick, E. 1956. *Perception and the representative design of psychological experiments.* 2nd ed. Berkeley: University of California Press.

Bryan, J. H., and Test, M. A. 1967. Models and helping: naturalistic studies in aiding behavior. *Journal of personality and social psychology* 6: 400–07.

Calkins, M. 1930. Mary Whiton Calkins. In *A history of psychology in autobiography,* vol. 1, ed. C. Murchison, pp. 31–62. Worcester, Mass.; Clark University Press.

Capra, P. C., and Dittes, J. E. 1962. Birth order as a selective force among volunteer subjects. *Journal of abnormal and social psychology* 64: 302.

Cason, H. 1934. The role of verbal activities and the conditioning of human subjects. *Psychological review* 41: 563–71.

Cason, H., and Cason, E. B. 1925. Association tendencies and learning ability. *Journal of experimental psychology* 8: 167–89.

Cattell, J. M. 1904. The conceptions and methods of psychology. *Popular science monthly* 66: 176–86.

Chapman, L. J.; Chapman, J. P.; and Brelje, T. 1969. Influence of the experimenter on pupillary dilation to sexually provocative pictures. *Journal of abnormal psychology* 74: 396–400.

Chertkoff, J. M., and Conley, M. 1967. Opening offer and frequency of concession as bargaining strategies. *Journal of personality and social psychology* 7: 181–84.

Clark, K. E. 1967. The invasion of privacy in the investigation of human behavior. Paper read at the meeting of the Eastern Psychological Association, Boston, Mass.

Cook, S. W., and Harris, R. E. 1937. The verbal conditioning of the galvanic skin reflex. *Journal of experimental psychology* 21: 202–10.

Cook, S.; Kimble, G. A.; Hicks, L. H.; McGuire, W. J.; Schoggen, P. H.; and Smith, M. B. 1971. Ethical standards for psychological research. *APA monitor* 2 (July): 9–28.

Cook, T. D.; Bean, J. R.; Calder, B. J.; Frey, R.; Krovetz, M. L.; and Reisman, S. R. 1970. Demand characteristics and three conceptions of the frequently deceived subject. *Journal of personality and social psychology* 14: 185–94.

Cox, D. E., and Sipprelle, C. N. 1971. Coercion in participation as a research subject. *American psychologist* 26: 726–28.

Crutchfield, R. S., and Krech, D. 1962. Some guides to the understanding of the history of psychology. In *Psychology in the making,* ed. L. Postman, pp. 3–27. New York: Knopf.

Deutsch, M.; Canavan, D.; and Rubin, J. 1971. Effects of size of conflict and sex of experimenter upon interpersonal bargaining. *Journal of experimental social psychology* 7: 258–67.

Deutsch, M.; and Krauss, R. M. 1960. The effect of threat on interpersonal bargaining. *Journal of abnormal and social psychology* 61: 181–89.

Dixon, P., and Oakes, W. 1965. Effect of intertrial activity on the relationship between awareness and verbal operant conditioning. *Journal of experimental psychology* 69: 152–57.

Dodge, R. 1912. The theory and limitations of introspection. *American journal of psychology* 23: 214–29.

Duncan, S.; Rosenberg, M.; and Finkelstein, J. 1969. The paralanguage of experimenter bias. *Sociometry* 32: 207–19.

References

Duncan, S., and Rosenthal, R. 1968. Vocal emphasis in experimenters' instruction reading as unintended determinant of subjects' responses. *Language and speech* 11: 20–26.

Earn, B. 1971. The subject in psychological experiments: effects of experimentally induced subject role expectations on performance. Unpublished manuscript. University of Toronto, Toronto, Canada.

Eisenman, R. 1970. Critique of "Treatment of insomnia by relaxation training": relaxation training, Rogerian therapy, or demand characteristics? *Journal of abnormal psychology* 75: 315–16.

Evans, F. J., and Orne, M. T. 1971. The disappearing hypnotist: the use of simulating subjects to evaluate how subjects perceive experimental procedures. *International journal of clinical and experimental hypnosis* 19: 277–96.

Feldman, R. E. 1968. Response to compatriot and foreigner who seek assistance. *Journal of personality and social psychology* 10: 202–14.

Fernberger, S. W. 1922. Behavior versus introspective psychology. *Psychological review* 29: 409–13.

———. 1937. A psychological cycle. *American journal of psychology* 50: 207–17.

Festinger, L.; Riecken, H. W., Jr.; Schachter, S. 1956. *When prophecy fails.* Minneapolis: University of Minnesota Press.

Freedman, J. L. 1969. Role playing: psychology by consensus. *Journal of personality and social psychology* 13: 107–14.

Friedman, N. 1967. *The social nature of psychological research: the psychological experiment as a social interaction.* New York: Basic Books.

Friedman, N.; Kurland, D.; and Rosenthal, R. 1965. Experimenter behavior as an unintended determinant of experimental results. *Journal of projective techniques and personality assessment* 29: 479–90.

Goldberg, P. A. 1965. Expectancy, choice, and the other person. *Journal of personality and social psychology* 2: 895–97.

Goldstein, A. P. 1962. *Therapist-patient expectancies in psychotherapy.* New York: Pergamon Press.

Greenberg, M. S. 1967. Role playing: an alternative to deception? *Journal of personality and social psychology* 7: 152–57.

Greenspoon, J. 1955. The reinforcing effect of two spoken sounds on the frequency of two responses. *American journal of psychology* 68: 409–16.

Greenspoon, J., and Brownstein, A. J. 1967. Awareness in verbal conditioning. *Journal of experimental research in personality* 2: 295–308.

Guetzkow, H.; Alger, C. F.; Brody, R. A.; Noel, R. C.; and Snyder, R. C. 1963. *Simulation in international relations.* Englewood Cliffs, N. J.: Prentice-Hall.

Gustav, A. 1962. Students' attitudes toward compulsory participation in experiments. *Journal of psychology* 53: 119–25.

Hamilton, D. L.; Thompson, J. J.; and White, A. M. 1970. Role of awareness and intentions in observational learning. *Journal of personality and social psychology* 16: 689–94.

Harris, S. 1971. Influence of subject and experimenter sex in psychological research. *Journal of consulting and clinical psychology* 37: 291–94.

Harris, S., and Masling, J. 1970. Examiner sex, subject sex, and Rorschach productivity. *Journal of consulting and clinical psychology* 34: 60–63.

Hicks, R. G. 1970. Experimenter effects on the physiological experiment. *Psychophysiology* 7: 10–17.

Holland, J.; Masling, J.; and Copley, D. 1970. Mental illness in lower class normal, obese and hyperobese women. *Psychosomatic medicine* 32: 351–57.

Holmes, D. S. 1967. Amount of experience in experiments as a determinant of perfomance in later experiments. *Journal of personality and social psychology* 7: 403–07.

Holmes, D. S., and Appelbaum, A. S. 1970. Nature of prior experimental experience as a determinant of performance in a subsequent experiment. *Journal of personality and social psychology* 14: 195–202.

Holmes, D. S., and Jorgensen, B. W. 1971. Do personality and social psychologists study men more than women? *Representative research in social psychology* 2: 71–76.

Holmes, J. G., and Strickland, L. H. 1970. Choice, freedom and confirmation of incentive expectancy as determinants of attitude change. *Journal of personality and social psychology* 14: 39–45.

Horowitz, I. A., and Rothschild, B. H. 1970. Conformity as a function of deception and role playing. *Journal of personality and social psychology* 14: 224–26.

Hull, C. 1930–1931. Quantitative methods of investigating hypnotic suggestion. Part II. *Journal of abnormal and social psychology* 25: 390–417.

Hyman, H. H. 1954. *Interviewing in social research*. Chicago: University of Chicago Press.

Jackson, C. W., Jr., and Pollard, J. C. 1966. Some nondeprivation variables which influence the "effects" of experimental sensory deprivation. *Journal of abnormal psychology* 71: 383–88.

Jacoby, J.; Olson, J. C.; and Haddock, R. A. 1971. Price, brand names and product composition characteristics as determinants of perceived quality. *Journal of applied psychology* 55: 570–79.

Johnson, E. S. 1967. The computer as experimenter. *Behavioral science* 12: 484–89.

Johnson, R. W. 1970. Subject performance as affected by experimenter expectancy, sex of experimenter, and verbal reinforcement. *Canadian journal of behavioral science* 2: 60–66.

Johnson, R. W., and Adair, J. G. 1970. The effects of systematic recording error vs. experimenter bias on latency of word association. *Journal of experimental research in personality* 4: 270–75.

———. 1972. Experimenter expectancy vs. systematic recording error under automated and non-automated stimulus presentation. *Journal of experimental research in personality* 6: 88–94.

Jung, J. 1969. Current practices and problems in use of college students for psychological research. *Canadian psychologist* 10: 280–90.

Kelman, H. C. 1967. Human use of human subjects: the problem of deception in social psychological experiments. *Psychological bulletin* 67: 1–11.

King, D. J. 1970. The subject pool. *American psychologist* 25: 1179–81.

Levy, L. H. 1967. Awareness, learning and the beneficent subject as expert witness. *Journal of personality and social psychology* 6: 365–70.

Lipmann, O. 1931. Uber eine Organisation zur Beschaffung Psychologishe auswertbaren Massen- und Gruppen-materials. *Psychoteclinische Zeitgschrift* 6: 190–91.

Littig, L., and Waddell, C. 1967. Sex and experimenter interaction in serial learning. *Journal of verbal learning and verbal behavior* 6: 676–78.

Lord, E. 1950. Experimentally induced variations in Rorschach performance. *Psychological monographs* 64, no. 10.

Lowin, A., and Ingraham, M. M. 1968. On lasting effects of deceptions. Paper presented at the meeting of the Midwestern Psychological Association, Chicago.

Lundwall, L., and Baekeland, F. 1971. Disulfiram treatment of alcoholism: review. *Journal of nervous and mental disease* 153: 381–94.

Lyons, J. 1964. On the psychology of the psychological experiment. In *Cognition: theory, research, promise*, ed. C. Scheerer, pp. 89–109. New York: Harper & Row.

McClelland, D. C. 1955. *Studies in motivation*. New York: Appleton-Century-Crofts.

McGuigan, F. J. 1963. The experimenter: a neglected stimulus object. *Psychological bulletin* 60: 421–28.

McGuire, W. J. 1967. Some impending reorientations in social psychology: some thoughts provoked by Kenneth Ring. *Journal of experimental social psychology* 3: 124–39.

McKinney, A. C. 1955. Deceiving experimental subjects. *American psychologist* 10: 133.

Marwit, S. J., and Marcia, J. E. 1967. Tester bias and response to projective instruments. *Journal of consulting psychology* 31: 253–58.

Masling, J. 1965. Differential indoctrination of examiners and Rorschach responses. *Journal of consulting psychology* 29: 198–201.

——. 1966. Role-related behavior of the subject and psychologist and its effects upon psychological data. In *Nebraska symposium on motivation*, ed. D. Levine, pp. 67–103. Lincoln, Neb.: University of Nebraska Press.

Masling, J., and Harris, S. 1969. Sexual aspects of TAT administration. *Journal of consulting and clinical psychology* 33: 166–69.

Melei, J. P., and Hilgard, E. R. 1964. Attitudes toward hypnosis, self-predictions, and hypnotic susceptibility. *International journal of clinical and experimental hypnosis* 12: 99–108.

Menges, R. J. 1971. The required subject pool: modifying student learning and attitudes. *Teaching of psychology newsletter*, March 1971, pp. 4, 7.

Miller, B. A.; Pokorny, A. D.; Valles, J.; and Cleveland, S. E. 1970. Biased sampling in alcoholism treatment research. *Quarterly journal of studies on alcohol* 31: 97–107.

Miller, N., and Bugelski, B. R. 1948. Minor studies of aggression: II. The influence of frustration as imposed by the ingroup on attitudes expressed toward outgroups. *Journal of psychology* 25: 437–42.

Minor, M. W. 1970. Experimenter-expectancy effect as a function of evaluation apprehension. *Journal of personality and social psychology* 15: 326–32.

Moll, A. 1898. *Hypnotism.* 4th ed. New York: Scribners.

Mondy, L. W. 1968. Degrees of awareness and intentions to comply in verbal conditioning. *Psychological reports* 22: 339–43.

Montanelli, D. S., and Hill, K. T. 1969. Children's achievement expectations and performance as a function of two consecutive reinforcement experiences, sex of subject, and sex of experimenter. *Journal of personality and social psychology* 13: 115–28.

Oakes, W. F. 1967. Verbal operant conditioning, intertrial activity, awareness, and the extended interview. *Journal of personality and social psychology* 6: 198–202.

Orne, M. T. 1962. On the social psychology of the psychological experiment: with particular reference to demand characteristics and their implications. *American psychologist* 17: 776–83.

———. 1969. Demand characteristics and the concept of quasi-controls. In *Artifact in behavioral research,* ed. R. Rosenthal and R. L. Rosnow, pp. 143–79. New York: Academic Press.

———. 1970. Hypnosis, motivation and the ecological validity of the psychological experiment. In *Nebraska symposium on motivation,* ed. W. J. Arnold and M. M. Page, pp. 187–265. Lincoln, Neb.: University of Nebraska Press.

Orne, M. T., and Scheibe, K. E. 1964. The contribution of nondeprivation factors in the production of sensory deprivation effects: the psychology of the "panic-button." *Journal of abnormal and social psychology* 68: 3–12.

Orne, M. T.; Sheehan, P. W.; and Evans, F. J. 1968. Occurrence of posthypnotic behavior outside the experimental setting. *Journal of personality and social psychology* 9: 189–96.

Page, M. M. 1968. Modification of figure-ground perception as a function of awareness of demand characteristics. *Journal of personality and social psychology* 9: 59–66.

———. 1969. The social psychology of a classical conditioning of attitudes experiment. *Journal of personality and social psychology* 11: 177–86.

———. 1970. Demand awareness, subject sophistication and the effectiveness of a verbal "reinforcement." *Journal of personality* 38: 287–301.

Page, M. M., and Scheidt, R. J. 1971. The elusive weapons effect: demand awareness, evaluation apprehension, and slightly sophisticated subjects. *Journal of personality and social psychology* 20: 304–09.

Page, S. 1971. The social psychology of research: attitudes and practices of psychologists. Unpublished manuscript. Lakeshore Psychiatric Hospital, Toronto, Canada.

Paulus, P. B., and Murdoch, P. 1971. Anticipated evaluation and audience presence in enhancement of dominant responses. *Journal of experimental social psychology* 7: 280–91.

Pillsbury, W. B. 1922. Suggestion for a compromise of existing controversies in psychology. *Psychological review* 29: 259–66.

Postman, L., and Jarrett, R. F. 1952. An experimental analysis of learning without awareness. *American journal of psychology* 65: 244–55.

Rapoport, A., and Chammah, A. M. 1965. Sex differences in factors contributing to the level of cooperation in the prisoner's dilemma game. *Journal of personality and social psychology* 2: 831–38.

Riecken, H. W. 1962. A program for research on experiments in social psychology. In *Decisions, values and groups*. vol. 2, ed. N. F. Washburne, pp. 25–41. New York: Pergamon Press.

Riegel, K. F.; Riegel, R. M.; and Meyer, G. A. 1967. A study of the dropout rates in longitudinal research on aging and the prediction of death. *Journal of personality and social psychology* 5: 342–48.

Ring, K. 1967. Experimental social psychology: some sober questions about some frivolous values. *Journal of experimental social psychology* 3: 113–23.

Rose, C. H. 1965. Representativeness of volunteer subjects in a longitudinal aging study. *Human development* 8: 152–56.

Rosenberg, M. J. 1965. When dissonance fails: on eliminating evaluation apprehension from attitude measurement. *Journal of personality and social psychology* 1: 28–42.

——. 1969. The conditions and consequences of evaluation apprehension. In *Artifact in behavioral research,* R. Rosenthal and R. L. Rosnow, pp. 280–349. New York: Academic Press.

Rosenfeld, H. M., and Baer, D. M. 1969. Unnoticed verbal conditioning of an aware experimenter by a more aware subject: the double-agent effect. *Psychological review* 76: 425–32.

——. 1970. Unbiased and unnoticed verbal conditioning – double agent robot procedure. *Journal of the experimental analysis of behavior* 14: 99–105.

Rosenthal, D., and Frank, J. D. 1956. Psychotherapy and the placebo effect. *Psychological bulletin* 53: 294–302.

Rosenthal, R. 1965. The volunteer subject. *Human relations* 18: 389–406.

——. 1966. *Experimenter effects in behavioral research.* New York: Appleton-Century-Crofts.

——. 1967. Covert communication and tacit understanding in the psychological experiment. *Psychological bulletin* 67: 356–67.

——. 1968. Experimenter expectancy and the reassuring nature of the null hypothesis decision procedure. *Psychological bulletin monograph supplement* 70: 30–47.

——. 1969a. Interpersonal expectations: effects of the experimenter's hypothesis. In *Artifact in behavioral research,* ed. R. Rosenthal and R. L. Rosnow, pp. 186–94. New York: Academic Press.

——. 1969*b.* Unintended effects of the clinical interaction: a taxonomy and a review of clinician expectancy effects. *Australian journal of psychology* 21: 1–20.

Rosenthal, R., and Fode, K. 1963. Psychology of the scientist. V. Three experiments in experimenter bias. *Psychological reports* 12: 491–511.

Rosenthal, R.; Fode, K.; Friedman, C.; and Vikan-Kline, L. 1960. Subjects' perception of their experimenter under conditions of experimenter bias. *Perceptual and motor skills* 11: 325–31.

Rosenthal, R., and Jacobson, L. 1968. *Pygmalion in the classroom.* New York: Holt, Rinehart and Winston.

Rosenthal, R.; Persinger, G. W.; Vikan-Kline, L.; and Mulry, R. C. 1963. The role of the research assistant in the mediation of experimenter bias. *Journal of personality* 31: 313–35.

Rosenthal, R., and Rosnow, R. L. 1969. The volunteer subject. In *Artifact in behavioral research,* ed. R. Rosenthal and R. L. Rosnow, pp. 59–118. New York: Academic Press.

Rosenzweig, S. 1933. The experimental situation as a psychological problem. *Psychological review* 40: 337–54.

——. 1952. The investigation of repression as an instance of experimental idiodynamics. *Psychological review* 59: 339–45.

——. 1970. E. G. Boring and the Zeitgeist: Eruditione gesta beavit. *Journal of psychology* 75: 59–71.

Rosnow, R. L., and Rosenthal, R. 1966. Volunteer subjects as the results of opinion change studies. *Psychological reports* 19: 1183–87.

——. 1970. Volunteer effects in behavioral research. *New directions in psychology,* vol. 4, pp. 213–77. New York: Holt, Rinehart and Winston.

Sattler, J. M. 1970. Racial "experimenter effects" in experimentation, testing, interviewing, and psychotherapy. *Psychological bulletin* 73: 137–60.

Schachter, S. 1959. *The psychology of affiliation.* Stanford, Calif.: Stanford University Press.

Schultz, D. P. 1969. The human subject in psychological research. *Psychological bulletin* 72: 214–28.

Schwitzgebel, R. K., and Traugott, M. 1968. Initial note on the placebo effect of machines. *Behavioral science* 13: 267–73.

Segal, M. H. 1965. Anthropology and psychology. In *Perspectives in social psychology,* ed. O. Klineberg and R. Christie, pp. 53–74. New York: Holt, Rinehart and Winston.

Sermat, V. 1970. Is game behavior related to behavior in other interpersonal situations? *Journal of personality and social psychology* 16: 92–109.

Shames, M., and Adair, J. G. 1967. Experimenter bias as a function of the type and structure of the task. *Canadian psychologist* 8: 176.

Sidis, B. 1906. Are there hypnotic hallucinations? *Psychological review* 13: 239–59.

Sigall, H.; Aronson, E.; and Van Hoose, T. 1970. The cooperative subject: myth or reality? *Journal of experimental social psychology* 6: 1–10.

Silverman, I. 1968a. Role related behavior of subjects in laboratory studies of attitude change. *Journal of personality and social psychology* 8: 343–48.

———. 1968b. The effects of experimenter outcome expectancy on latency of word association. *Journal of clinical psychology* 24: 60–63.

———. 1971. Crisis in social psychology: relevance of relevance. *American psychologist* 26: 583–84.

Silverman, I., and Kleinman, D. 1967. A response deviance interpretation of the effects of experimentally induced frustration on prejudice. *Journal of experimental research in personality* 2: 150–53.

Silverman, I., and Shulman, A. D. 1970. A conceptual model of artifact in attitude change studies. *Sociometry* 33: 97–107.

Silverman, I.; Shulman, A. D.; and Wiesenthal, D. L. 1970. Effects of deceiving and debriefing psychological subjects on performance in later experiments. *Journal of personality and social psychology* 14: 203–12.

Smart, R. 1966. Subject selection bias in psychological research. *Canadian psychologist* 7: 115–21.

Speer, D. C., and Zold, A. 1971. An example of self-selection bias in follow-up research. *Journal of clinical psychology* 27: 64–68.

Spielberger, C. D. 1962. The role of awareness in verbal conditioning. *Journal of personality* 30: 73–101.

Spielberger, C. D., and DeNike, L. D. 1966. Descriptive behaviorism versus cognitive theory in verbal operant conditioning. *Psychological review* 73: 306–26.

Staats, A. 1969. Experimental demand characteristics and the classical conditioning of attitudes. *Journal of personality and social psychology* 11: 187–92.

Staats, A. W., and Staats, C. K. 1958. Attitudes established by classical conditioning. *Journal of abnormal and social psychology* 57: 37–40.

Stricker, L. J. 1967. The true deceiver. *Psychological bulletin* 68: 13–20.

Stricker, L. J.; Messick, S.; and Jackson, D. N. 1967. Suspicion of deception: implications for conformity research. *Journal of personality and social psychology* 5: 379–89.

———. 1969. Evaluating deception in psychological research. *Psychological bulletin* 71: 343–51.

Taffel, C. 1955. Anxiety and the conditioning of verbal behavior. *Journal of abnormal and social psychology* 51: 496–501.

Thibault, J. W., and Kelley, H. H. 1959. *The social psychology of groups.* New York: Wiley.

Thorndike, E. L., and Rock, R. T. 1934. Learning without awareness of what is being learned or intent to learn it. *Journal of experimental psychology* 17: 1–19.

Titchener, E. B. 1895. The type-theory of the simple reaction. *Mind* 4: 506–14.

———. 1912. Prolegomena to a study of introspection. *American journal of psychology* 23: 427–48.

Vernon, P. E. 1934. The attitude of the subject in personality testing. *Journal of applied psychology* 18: 165–77.

Videbeck, R., and Bates, H. D. 1966. Verbal conditioning by a simulated experimenter. *Psychological record* 16: 145–52.

Watson, J. B. 1913. Psychology as the behaviorist views it. *Psychological review* 20: 158–77.

Webb, E. J.; Campbell, D. T.; Schwartz, R. D.; Seechrest, L. 1966. *Unobtrusive measures: nonreactive research in the social sciences.* Chicago: Rand McNally.

Weber, S. J., and Cook, T. D. 1972. Subject effects in laboratory research: an examination of subject roles, demand characteristics, and valid inference. *Psychological bulletin* 77: 273–95.

Weissman, L.; Moore, J. D.; Thomas, G. B.; and Whitman, E. N. 1972. Personality factors in prison volunteers related to response in clinical drug trials. *Journal of clinical pharmacology and journal of new drugs* 12: 5–10.

Wheeler, R. H. 1929. *The science of psychology.* New York: T. Y. Crowell.

Willis, R. H., and Willis, Y. A. 1970. Role playing versus deception: an experimental comparison. *Journal of personality and social psychology* 16: 472–77.

Winkel, G. H., and Sarason, I. G. 1964. Subject, experimenter and situational variables in research on anxiety. *Journal of abnormal and social psychology* 68: 601–08.

Wodehouse, H. 1931. On the discernment of the disciplinary value of studies. *British journal of educational psychology* 1: 41–47.

Wolfensberger, W. 1967. Ethical issues in research with human subjects. *Science* 155: 47–51.

Woodworth, R. S. 1924. Four varieties of behaviorism. *Psychological review* 31: 257–64.

Wrightsman, L. S. 1969. Wallace supporters and adherence to "law and order." *Journal of personality and social psychology* 13: 17–22.

For the past fifty years, one fundamental aspect of the methodology of psychology has resisted evolution and growth — the relationship of the human subject to the psychological experiment. Adopting the natural science model of the experimental method, we have regarded the interaction of subject, experimenter, and study as fixed and the laboratory as a methodologically sterile setting for the study of behavior. Recent research on the social psychology of the psychological experiment has proved us wrong.

Research has revealed "social contamination" in the laboratory; the subject and experimenter provide a stimulus for each other, their respective attitudes, feelings, and expectations influencing the data that are collected. This research has proposed ways to control or measure subject and experimenter bias in a study as well as alternatives to the traditional laboratory experiment. Because of its diversity, however, it is not easily interpretable, and its implications for methodological changes are not clear. This book provides an integrated view of this research and speculates on its implications for future experimentation. It is hoped that readers will gain from it a mature understanding of the experimental process, concern for its human element, and an appreciation of some of the unique controls they must exercise.

— From the Preface

Little, Brown and Company   Boston   007005